Teach Yourself
Computers & the Internet 2nd Edition

IDG's **3-D Visual** Series

IDG BOOKS

From **maranGraphics**

IDG Books Worldwide, Inc.
An International Data Group Company
Foster City, CA • Indianapolis • Chicago • Southlake, TX

Teach Yourself Computers & the Internet VISUALLY™, 2nd Edition

Published by
IDG Books Worldwide, Inc.
An International Data Group Company
919 E. Hillsdale Blvd., Suite 400
Foster City, CA 94404

Library of Congress Catalog Card No.: 98-72811

ISBN: 0-7645-6041-7

Printed in the United States of America
10 9 8

Distributed in the United States by IDG Books Worldwide, Inc.

Distributed by Transworld Publishers Limited in the United Kingdom; by IDG Norge Books for Norway; by IDG Sweden Books for Sweden; by Woodslane Pty. Ltd. for Australia; by Woodslane (NZ) Ltd. for New Zealand; by Addison Wesley Longman Singapore Pte Ltd. for Singapore, Malaysia, Thailand, Indonesia and Korea; by Norma Comunicaciones S.A. for Colombia; by Intersoft for South Africa; by International Thomson Publishing for Germany, Austria and Switzerland; by Toppan Company Ltd. for Japan; by Distribuidora Cuspide for Argentina; by Livraria Cultura for Brazil; by Ediciencia S.A. for Ecuador; by Ediciones ZETA S.C.R. Ltda. for Peru; by WS Computer Publishing Corporation, Inc., for the Philippines; by Unalis Corporation for Taiwan; by Contemporanea de Ediciones for Venezuela; by Computer Book & Magazine Store for Puerto Rico; by Express Computer Distributors for the Caribbean and West Indies. Authorized Sales Agent: Anthony Rudkin Associates for the Middle East and North Africa.
For corporate orders, please call maranGraphics at 800-469-6616.
For general information on IDG Books Worldwide's books in the U.S., please call our Consumer Customer Service department at 800-762-2974.
For reseller information, including discounts and premium sales, please call our Reseller Customer Service department at 800-434-3422.
For information on where to purchase IDG Books Worldwide's books outside the U.S., please contact our International Sales department at 650-655-3200 or fax 650-655-3297.
For information on foreign language translations, please contact our Foreign & Subsidiary Rights department at 650-655-3021 or fax 650-655-3281.
For sales inquiries and special prices for bulk quantities, please contact our Sales department at 650-655-3200.
For information on using IDG Books Worldwide's books in the classroom or for ordering examination copies, please contact our Educational Sales department at 800-434-2086 or fax 317-596-5499.
For press review copies, author interviews, or other publicity information, please contact our Public Relations department at 650-655-3000 or fax 650-655-3299.
For authorization to photocopy items for corporate, personal, or educational use, please contact maranGraphics at 800-469-6616.

Trademark Acknowledgments

©1998 maranGraphics, Inc.

The 3-D illustrations are the copyright of maranGraphics, Inc.

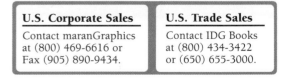

U.S. Corporate Sales	**U.S. Trade Sales**
Contact maranGraphics at (800) 469-6616 or Fax (905) 890-9434.	Contact IDG Books at (800) 434-3422 or (650) 655-3000.

Welcome to the world of IDG Books Worldwide.

IDG Books Worldwide, Inc., is a subsidiary of International Data Group, the world's largest publisher of computer-related information and the leading global provider of information services on information technology. IDG was founded more than 25 years ago and now employs more than 8,500 people worldwide. IDG publishes more than 270 computer publications in over 75 countries (see listing below). More than 90 million people read one or more IDG publications each month.

Launched in 1990, IDG Books Worldwide is today the #1 publisher of best-selling computer books in the United States. We are proud to have received eight awards from the Computer Press Association in recognition of editorial excellence and three from Computer Currents' First Annual Readers' Choice Awards. Our best-selling ...For Dummies® series has more than 25 million copies in print with translations in 30 languages. IDG Books Worldwide, through a joint venture with IDG's Hi-Tech Beijing, became the first U.S. publisher to publish a computer book in the People's Republic of China. In record time, IDG Books Worldwide has become the first choice for millions of readers around the world who want to learn how to better manage their businesses.

Our mission is simple: Every one of our books is designed to bring extra value and skill-building instructions to the reader. Our books are written by experts who understand and care about our readers. The knowledge base of our editorial staff comes from years of experience in publishing, education, and journalism - experience which we use to produce books for the '90s. In short, we care about books, so we attract the best people. We devote special attention to details such as audience, interior design, use of icons, and illustrations. And because we use an efficient process of authoring, editing, and desktop publishing our books electronically, we can spend more time ensuring superior content and spend less time on the technicalities of making books.

You can count on our commitment to deliver high-quality books at competitive prices on topics you want to read about. At IDG Books Worldwide, we continue in the IDG tradition of delivering quality for more than 25 years. You'll find no better book on a subject than one from IDG Books Worldwide.

John Kilcullen
President and CEO
IDG Books Worldwide, Inc.

IDG Books Worldwide, Inc., is a subsidiary of International Data Group, the world's largest publisher of computer-related information and the leading global provider of information services on information technology. International Data Group publishes over 276 computer publications in over 75 countries. Ninety million people read one or more International Data Group publications each month. International Data Group's publications include: Argentina: Annuario de Informatica, Computerworld Argentina, PC World Argentina; Australia: Australian Macworld, Client/Server Journal, Computer Living, Computerworld, Computerworld 100, Digital News, IT Casebook, Network World, On-line World Australia, PC World, Publishing Essentials, Reseller, WebMaster; Austria: Computerwelt Österreich, Networks Austria, PC Tip; Belarus: PC World Belarus; Belgium: Data News; Brazil: Annuario de Informatica, Computerworld Brazil, Connections, Super Game Power, Macworld, PC Player, PC World Brazil, Publish Brazil, Reseller News; Bulgaria: Computerworld Bulgaria, Networkworld/Bulgaria, PC & MacWorld Bulgaria; Canada: CIO Canada, Client/Server World, Computerworld Canada, InfoCanada, Network World Canada; Chile: Computerworld Chile, PC World Chile; Colombia: Computerworld Colombia, PC World Colombia; Costa Rica: PC World Centro America; The Czech and Slovak Republics: Computerworld Czechoslovakia, Elektronika Czechoslovakia, Macworld Czech Danmark, PC World Danmark Supplements, TECH World; Dominican Republic: PC World Republica Dominicana; Ecuador: PC World Ecuador; Egypt: Computerworld Middle East, PC World Middle East; El Salvador: PC World Centro America; Finland: MikroPC, Tietoverkko, Tietoviikko; France: Distributique, Golden, Hebdo-Distributique, Info PC, Le Guide du Monde Informatique, Le Monde Informatique, Reseaux & Telecoms; Germany: Computer Partner, Computerwoche, Computerwoche Extra, Computerwoche Focus, I/M Information Management, Macwelt, PC Welt; Greece: GamePro, Multimedia World; Guatemala: PC World Centro America; Honduras: PC World Centro America; Hong Kong: Computerworld Hong Kong, PCWorld Hong Kong, Publish in Asia; Hungary: ABCD CD-ROM, Computerworld Szamitastechnika, PC & Mac World Hungary, PC-X Magazine; Iceland: Tolvuheimur/PC World Island; India: Information Systems Computerworld, PC World India, Publish in Asia; Indonesia: InfoKomputer PC World, Komputek Computerworld, Publish in Asia; Ireland: ComputerScope, PC Live!; Israel: People & Computers; Italy: Computerworld Italia, Computerworld Italia Special Editions, Macworld Italia, Networking Italia, PC Shopping, PC World Italia, PC World/Walt Disney; Japan: DTP World, HP Open World Japan, Macworld Japan, Nikkei Personal Computing, Open World Japan, OS/2 World Japan, SunWorld Japan, Windows World Japan; Kenya: East African Computer News; Korea: Hi-Tech Information/Computerworld, Macworld Korea, PC World Korea; Macedonia: PC World Macedonia; Malaysia: Computerworld Malaysia, PC World Malaysia, Publish in Asia; Mexico: Computerworld Mexico, Macworld, PC World Mexico; Myanmar: PC World Myanmar; Netherlands: Computer! Totaal, LAN Magazine, LanWorld Buyers Guide, Macworld, Net Magazine, Totaal! Beurskrant; New Zealand: Absolute Beginner's Guide, Computer Buyer, Computer Industry Directory, Computerworld New Zealand, MTB, Network World, PC World New Zealand; Nicaragua: PC World Centro America; Nigeria: PC World Nigeria; Norway: Computerworld Norge, Computerworld Privat (Datamagasinet), CW Rapport Norge, IDG's KURSGUIDE, Macworld Norge, Multimediaworld, PC World Ekspress, PC World Nettverk, PC World Norge, PC World's Produktguide, Windows World Spesial; Pakistan: Computerworld Pakistan, PC World Pakistan; Panama: PC World Panama; P. R. of China: China Computer Users, China Computerworld, China Infoworld, China Telecom World Weekly, Computer & Communication, Electronic Design China, Electronics Today, Electronics Weekly, Game Camp, Game Soft, Network World China, PC World China, Popular Computer Weekly, Software Weekly, Software World, Telecom World; Peru: Computerworld Peru, PC World Profesional Peru, PC World Peru; Poland: Computerworld Poland, Computerworld Special Report, Macworld, Networld, PC World Komputer; Philippines: Computerworld Philippines, PC World Philippines, Publish in Asia; Portugal: Cerebro/PC World, Computerworld/Correio Informático, Dealer World Portugal, Mac*In/PC*In, Multimedia World Portugal; Puerto Rico: PC World Puerto Rico; Romania: Computerworld Romania, PC World Romania, Telecom Romania; Russia: Computerworld Russia, Mir PK, Sety; Singapore: Computerworld Singapore, PC World Singapore, Publish in Asia; Slovenia: MONITOR; South Africa: Computing S.A., InfoWorld S.A., Network World S.A., Software World; Spain: Computerworld Espa-a, COMUNICACIONES WORLD, Dealer World, Macworld Espa-a, PC World Espa-a; Sweden: CAP&Design, Computer Sweden, Corporate Computing, MacWorld, Maxi Data, MikroDatorn, Nätverk & Kommunikation, PC/Aktiv, PC World, Windows World; Switzerland: Computerworld Schweiz, Macworld Schweiz, PCtip; Taiwan: Computerworld Taiwan, Macworld Taiwan, PC World Taiwan, Publish Taiwan, Windows World; Thailand: Thai Computerworld, Publish in Asia; Turkey: Computerworld Turkiye, MACWORLD Turkiye, PC WORLD Turkiye; Ukraine: Computerworld Kiev, Computers & Software, Multimedia World Ukraine, PC World Ukraine; United Kingdom: Acorn User, Amiga Action, Amiga Computing, Appletalk, Computing, GamePro, Macworld, Network News, Parents and Computers, PC Advisor, PC Home, PSX Pro UK, The WEB; United States: Cable in the Classroom, CD Review, CIO Magazine, Computerworld, Computerworld Client/Server Journal, Digital Video Magazine, DOS World, Federal Computer Week, GamePro, InfoWorld, I-Way, JavaWorld, Macworld, Multimedia World, Netscape World Online, Network World, PC Entertainment, PC World, Publish, SunWorld Online, SWATPro Magazine, Video Event, WebMaster; Uruguay: PC World Uruguay; Venezuela: Computerworld Venezuela, PC World Venezuela; and Vietnam: PC World Vietnam.

Every maranGraphics book represents
the extraordinary vision and commitment of a unique family:
the Maran family of Toronto, Canada.

Back Row (from left to right):   Sherry Maran, Rob Maran, Richard Maran,
Maxine Maran, Jill Maran.

Front Row (from left to right):   Judy Maran, Ruth Maran.

Richard Maran is the company founder and its inspirational leader. He developed maranGraphics' proprietary communication technology called "visual grammar." This book is built on that technology—empowering readers with the easiest and quickest way to learn about computers.

Ruth Maran is the Author and Architect—a role Richard established that now bears Ruth's distinctive touch. She creates the words and visual structure that are the basis for the books.

Judy Maran is the Project Manager. She works with Ruth, Richard and the highly talented maranGraphics illustrators, designers and editors to transform Ruth's material into its final form.

Rob Maran is the Technical and Production Specialist. He makes sure the state-of-the-art technology used to create these books always performs as it should.

Sherry Maran manages the Reception, Order Desk and any number of areas that require immediate attention and a helping hand.

Jill Maran is a jack-of-all-trades who works in the Accounting and Human Resources department.

Maxine Maran is the Business Manager and family sage. She maintains order in the business and family—and keeps everything running smoothly.

CREDITS

Author:
Ruth Maran

Technical Updates:
Paul Whitehead
Robert Maran

Technical Editing Director:
Kelleigh Wing

Technical Editors:
Roxanne Van Damme
Jason M. Brown
Cathy Benn

Project Manager:
Judy Maran

Editors:
Raquel Scott
Janice Boyer
Michelle Kirchner
James Menzies
Frances LoPresti
Emmet Mellow

Layout Designer:
Treena Lees

Illustrators:
Russ Marini
Jamie Bell
Peter Grecco
Jeff Jones

Permissions Coordinator:
Jenn Hillman

Indexer:
Raquel Scott

Post Production:
Robert Maran

Editorial Support:
Michael Roney

ACKNOWLEDGMENTS

Thanks to the dedicated staff of maranGraphics, including
Jamie Bell, Cathy Benn, Janice Boyer, Jason M. Brown,
Francisco Ferreira, Peter Grecco, Jenn Hillman, Jeff Jones,
Michelle Kirchner, Wanda Lawrie, Treena Lees, Frances Lo Presti,
Michael W. MacDonald, Jill Maran, Judy Maran, Maxine Maran,
Robert Maran, Sherry Maran, Russ Marini, Emmet Mellow,
James Menzies, Raquel Scott, Roxanne Van Damme,
Paul Whitehead and Kelleigh Wing.

Finally, to Richard Maran who originated the easy-to-use
graphic format of this guide. Thank you for your inspiration
and guidance.

Permissions

Advanced Micro Devices

Copyright © 1998 Advanced Micro Devices, Inc. Reprinted with permission of copyright owner. All rights reserved.

AMD, the AMD logo, 3Dnow!, AMD-K6-2, AMD-K6-2 logo are trademarks of Advanced Micro Devices, Inc. and AMD-K6 is a registered trademark, and may not be used in advertising or publicity pertaining to distribution of this information without specific, written prior permission.

Apple Computer

Macintosh is a trademark of Apple Computers Inc., registered in the United States and other countries.

Cyber Patrol

© 1998 The Learning Company, Inc.

Cyrix

Cyrix is a registered trademark and M II and MediaGX are trademarks of Cyrix Corporation, a subsidiary of National Semiconductor Corporation.

Dell Computers

Dell is a registered trademark of Dell Computer Corporation.

ENERGY STAR

ENERGY STAR is a US registered mark.

Excite

Excite, Excite search and the Excite Logo are trademarks of Excite, Inc. and may be registered in various jurisdictions. Excite screen display copyright 1995-1998 Excite, Inc.

Imation

Travan is a trademark of Imation Corp.
SuperDisk, The SuperDisk logo, and the capability symbol are trademarks of Imation Corp.

Iomega

Copyright © 1998 Iomega Corporation. All rights reserved. Iomega, Zip and Jaz are registered trademarks of Iomega Corporation.

Microsoft

Screen shots reprinted with permission from Microsoft Corporation.

Motorola

Copyright © 1998 Motorola, Inc. Motorola, and the Motorola logo are registered trademarks of Motorola, Inc. PowerPC, the PowerPC logo, PowerPC 603e, PowerPC 604e, and PowerPC 750 are trademarks of IBM Corp. and are used by Motorola under license therefrom.

Netscape

Netscape Communications Corporation has not authorized, sponsored, or endorsed, or approved this publication and is not responsible for its contents. Netscape and the Netscape Communications Corporate Logos, are trademarks and trade names of Netscape Communications Corporation. All other product names and/or logos are trademarks of their respective owners.

Nexor

© Nexor LTD. Archie and ArchiePlex are trademarks of Nexor Ltd.

People Online

© 1998 Time Inc. New Media. All rights reserved. Reproduction in whole or in part without permission is prohibited. Pathfinder is a registered trademark of Time Inc. New Media.

Shareware

Reprinted with permission from CNET, Inc. copyright 1995-8 www.cnet.com

Trimark

Copyright of Trimark Pictures 1996.

USA Today

Copyright 1996 USA TODAY Online.

Wal-Mart

Copyright © 1998 Wal-Mart Stores, Inc.

WBS

WBS, WebChat®, and the WebChat Broadcasting System are trademarks of WebChat Communications, Inc. Copyright 1995-1998 by WebChat Communications, Inc. Infoseek Corporation. All rights reserved.

Yahoo!

Text and artwork copyright © 1996 by Yahoo!, Inc. All rights reserved. Yahoo! and the Yahoo! logo are trademarks of Yahoo!, Inc.

The following companies have also given us permission to use their screen shots, chips, etc.:

American Express
AOL
CNNSI
The Complete Works of Shakespeare
Fade to Black
Flower Stop
FTP
The Hall of Malls
Intel
Minolta
National Space Science Data Center
Online Vacation Mall
Ragu
The Sports Network
Sunkist
Symantec
SyQuest

TABLE OF CONTENTS

TABLE OF CONTENTS

Chapter 1

Introduction to Computers

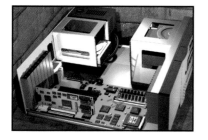

Chapter 2

Input and Output

Chapter 3
Processing

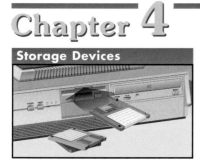

Chapter 4
Storage Devices

Chapter 5
Portable Computers

TABLE OF CONTENTS

Chapter 6

Software

Chapter 7

Operating Systems

Chapter 8

Macintosh Computers

Chapter 9

Networks

Chapter 10

The Internet

Chapter 11

The World Wide Web

TABLE OF CONTENTS

Chapter 12

Interesting Web Sites

Chapter 13

Electronic Mail

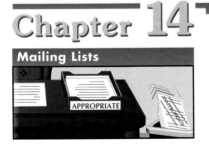

Chapter 14

Mailing Lists

Chapter 15

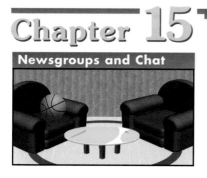

Newsgroups and Chat

Chapter 16

FTP

CHAPTER 1

Introduction to Computers

Need help using your new computer?
This chapter will help you get started.

HARDWARE AND SOFTWARE

Hardware and software are the two basic parts of a computer system.

Hardware is any part of a computer system you can see or touch.

Peripheral

A peripheral is any piece of hardware attached to a computer, such as a printer.

Software is a set of electronic instructions that tell a computer what to do. You cannot see or touch software, but you can see and touch the packaging the software comes in.

Application Software

Application software allows you to accomplish specific tasks. Popular application software includes Microsoft® Word and Intuit Quicken.

Operating System Software

Operating system software controls the overall activity of a computer. Most new computers come with the Windows 98 operating system software.

There are many ways to get help when using new hardware and software.

Documentation

Hardware and software should include documentation that tells you how to set up and use the product. Many software packages also come with a built-in help feature. You can also check local book stores for manuals with detailed, step-by-step instructions.

Call the Experts

If you have questions about setting up or using new hardware or software, try calling the store where you purchased the product.

Classes

Colleges and computer stores often offer computer courses. Many communities also have computer clubs where you can ask questions and exchange ideas.

HOW COMPUTERS WORK

A computer collects, processes, stores and outputs information.

Input

An input device lets you communicate with a computer. You can use input devices to enter information and issue commands. A keyboard, mouse and joystick are input devices.

Process

The Central Processing Unit (CPU) is the main chip in a computer. The CPU processes instructions, performs calculations and manages the flow of information through a computer system. The CPU communicates with input, output and storage devices to perform tasks.

Store

A storage device reads and records information on storage media. The computer uses information stored on the storage media to perform tasks. Popular examples of storage devices include a hard drive, floppy drive, CD-Recordable drive and tape drive.

Output

An output device lets a computer communicate with you. These devices display information on a screen, create printed copies or generate sound. A monitor, printer and speakers are output devices.

Bytes are used to measure the amount of information a device can store.

Byte

One byte is one character. A character can be a number, letter or symbol.

One byte consists of eight bits (binary digits). A bit is the smallest unit of information a computer can process.

Terabyte (TB)

One terabyte is 1,099,511,627,776 characters. This is approximately equal to an entire library of books.

Kilobyte (K)

One kilobyte is 1,024 characters. This is approximately equal to one page of double-spaced text.

Megabyte (MB)

One megabyte is 1,048,576 characters. This is approximately equal to one book.

Gigabyte (GB)

One gigabyte is 1,073,741,824 characters. This is approximately equal to a shelf of books in a library.

TYPES OF COMPUTER SYSTEMS

There are several types of computer systems.

PC (Personal Computer)

A PC is a computer designed to meet the needs of one person and usually refers to IBM-compatible computers. PCs are found in many businesses and are popular for home use.

Macintosh

Macintosh computers are found in many homes and are very popular in the graphics, publishing and multimedia industries. The Macintosh was the first home computer that offered a graphical display.

Mainframe

A mainframe is a computer that can process and store large amounts of information and support many users at the same time.

A terminal, consisting of a keyboard and monitor, is used to input and output information on a mainframe.

Set-top Box

A set-top box is a computer device that connects to your television. Set-top boxes allow you to use your telephone line or television cable connection to browse the Internet and exchange electronic mail on your television.

A TYPICAL COMPUTER

A typical computer system consists of several parts.

Computer Case

A computer case contains most of the major components of a computer system.

Monitor

A monitor is a device that displays text and images generated by the computer.

Printer

A printer is a device that produces a paper copy of documents you create on the computer.

Modem

A modem is a device that lets computers communicate through telephone lines. A modem can be found outside or inside the computer case.

Keyboard

A keyboard is a device that lets you type information and instructions into a computer.

Mouse

A mouse is a handheld device that lets you select and move items on the screen.

All computers contain the same basic components.

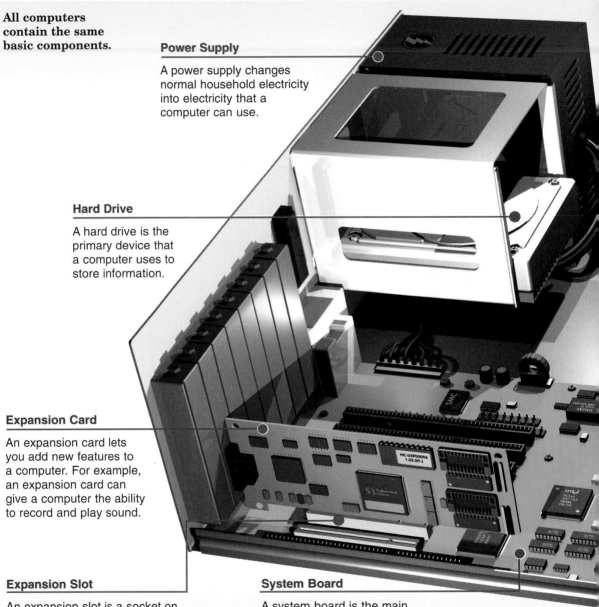

Power Supply

A power supply changes normal household electricity into electricity that a computer can use.

Hard Drive

A hard drive is the primary device that a computer uses to store information.

Expansion Card

An expansion card lets you add new features to a computer. For example, an expansion card can give a computer the ability to record and play sound.

Expansion Slot

An expansion slot is a socket on the system board. An expansion card plugs into an expansion slot.

System Board

A system board is the main circuit board of a computer. All electrical components plug into the system board.

Floppy Drive

A floppy drive stores and retrieves information on floppy disks.

Drive Bay

A drive bay is a space inside the computer case where a hard drive, floppy drive, CD-ROM drive or DVD-ROM drive sits.

CD-ROM or DVD-ROM Drive

A CD-ROM drive reads information stored on compact discs (CDs). A DVD-ROM drive reads information stored on CDs and DVD-ROM discs.

Random Access Memory (RAM)

RAM temporarily stores information inside a computer. This information is lost when you turn off the computer.

Central Processing Unit (CPU)

A CPU is the main chip in a computer. The CPU processes instructions, performs calculations and manages the flow of information through a computer.

COMPUTER CASE

A computer case contains all the major components of a computer system.

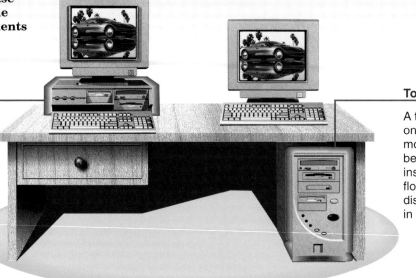

Desktop Case

A desktop case usually sits on a desk, under a monitor.

Tower Case

A tower case usually sits on the floor. This provides more desk space, but can be less convenient for inserting and removing floppy disks and CD-ROM discs. Tower cases come in different sizes.

All-in-one Case

An all-in-one case contains a monitor, disk drive, CD-ROM drive and speakers in a single unit.

Portable

A portable is a small, lightweight computer that you can easily transport. A portable has a built-in keyboard and screen.

A power supply changes the alternating current (AC) that comes from an outlet to the direct current (DC) that a computer can use.

A fan inside the power supply prevents the parts inside a computer from overheating.

The capacity of a power supply is measured in watts. An average computer uses up to 200 watts, whereas an average light bulb uses 60 watts.

PROTECT YOUR EQUIPMENT

Changes in electrical power can damage equipment and information.

Surge Protector

A surge protector, or surge suppressor, guards a computer against surges. A surge is a fluctuation in power. These fluctuations happen most often during storms.

UPS

An Uninterruptible Power Supply (UPS) protects a computer from a loss of power. A UPS contains a battery that stores electrical power. If the power fails, the battery can run the computer for a short time so you can save your information.

A port is a connector at the back of a computer where you plug in an external device such as a printer or modem. This allows instructions and data to flow between the computer and the device.

Parallel Port

A parallel port has 25 holes. This type of port is known as a female connector. A parallel port connects a printer or tape drive.

A computer internally labels each parallel port with the letters LPT. The first parallel port is named LPT1, the second parallel port is named LPT2, and so on.

There are two enhanced types of parallel ports— Enhanced Parallel Port (EPP) and Extended Capabilities Port (ECP). These types of parallel ports increase the speed at which information flows between the computer and a device.

Monitor Port

A monitor port connects a monitor.

Serial Port

A serial port has either 9 or 25 pins. This type of port is known as a male connector. A serial port connects a modem or mouse.

A computer internally labels each serial port with the letters COM. The first serial port is named COM1, the second serial port is named COM2, and so on.

Keyboard Port

A keyboard port connects a keyboard. Keyboard ports are available in two sizes.

Game Port

A game port connects a joystick.

USB Port

Universal Serial Bus (USB) is a type of port that allows you to connect up to 127 devices using only one port. For example, you can use a USB port to connect a printer, modem, joystick and scanner to your computer. Most new computers come with two USB ports.

An expansion card is a circuit board that lets you add a new feature to a computer.

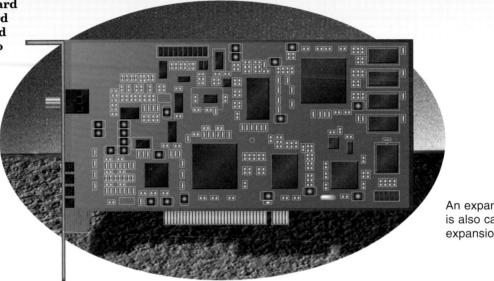

An expansion card is also called an expansion board.

Expansion Slot

An expansion slot is a socket where you plug in an expansion card.

The number of expansion slots your computer has indicates how many expansion cards you can add to the computer. Before you buy a computer, make sure it has enough empty expansion slots for your future needs.

Connect Devices

Some expansion cards are accessible from the back of a computer. These expansion cards contain ports where you can plug in devices. For example, you can plug speakers into a sound card to hear the sound generated by the computer.

TYPES OF EXPANSION CARDS

A computer usually comes with one or more expansion cards.

Video

A video card generates the images displayed on the monitor.

Modem

A modem card lets computers exchange information through telephone lines.

Sound

A sound card lets a computer play and record high-quality sound.

Networking

A network interface card lets connected computers share information and equipment.

PURCHASE A NEW COMPUTER

There are many factors to consider when purchasing a new computer.

Cost

The cost of a computer depends on your needs. You can purchase a basic home computer for under $1,000. If you want a computer better able to handle complex tasks, such as running multimedia applications, you will need to spend more money.

In most cases, a monitor is not included in the price of a computer.

Brand-name and Clone Computers

When purchasing a new computer, you can choose either a brand-name or a clone computer. Brand-name computers are made by large manufacturers, such as IBM or Dell. Clone computers are made by independent manufacturers. Clone computers function exactly like brand-name computers, but are usually less expensive.

After-sale Service

You should make sure the computer you purchase comes with after-sale service. After-sale service should include a one or two-year warranty on computer parts and labor, as well as telephone technical support.

You can upgrade a computer to enhance the computer's performance. For many upgrades, you will need the assistance of an experienced computer repairperson.

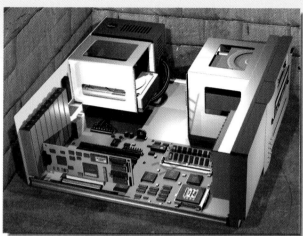

Upgrading usually refers to replacing an old or obsolete component with a newer component to improve the efficiency of the computer. Upgrading can also include adding a new component, such as a tape drive or DVD-ROM drive, to increase the capabilities of the computer.

CONSIDERATIONS

Cost

You should always determine the cost of an upgrade before performing the upgrade. If you are planning a major upgrade, such as replacing the system board or CPU, it may be less expensive to purchase a new computer.

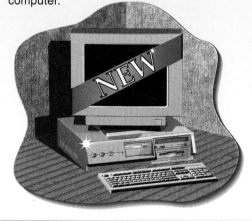

Effective Upgrades

Increasing the amount of memory in a computer is one of the most effective upgrades you can perform. Most computers should have at least 32 MB of memory.

ERGONOMICS

Ergonomics is the science of designing equipment for a safe and comfortable working environment.

You can avoid back and neck strain by ensuring that your chair provides proper support and by placing the monitor where you can comfortably view the screen.

Monitor Placement

The top edge of the monitor should be at eye level or slightly lower. You can use a monitor stand or telephone book to raise the monitor to the appropriate level on your desk.

Posture

When seated, make sure your feet are flat on the floor and you do not lean forward or slouch in your chair. You should shift positions often and stand up to stretch your arms and legs at least once an hour.

Chair

Look for a fully adjustable chair that provides support for your lower back. Contoured chair seats help blood circulate more freely by relieving pressure on the legs.

PREVENT WRIST STRAIN

You can avoid wrist strain when typing by keeping your elbows level with the keyboard and keeping your wrists straight and higher than your fingers.

Carpal Tunnel Syndrome (CTS)

Carpal Tunnel Syndrome is a Repetitive Stress Injury (RSI) whose symptoms include numbness, tingling and pain in the fingers. The condition affects some workers who type without proper wrist support or type for long periods of time without breaks.

Wrist Rest

You can use a wrist rest with your keyboard to elevate your wrists and ensure they remain straight at all times. Some mouse pads also come with built-in wrist rests.

Keyboard Shelf

You can use a keyboard shelf to help keep your elbows level with the keyboard. A keyboard shelf lets you adjust the height and position of the keyboard and slides under the desk to provide more desk space.

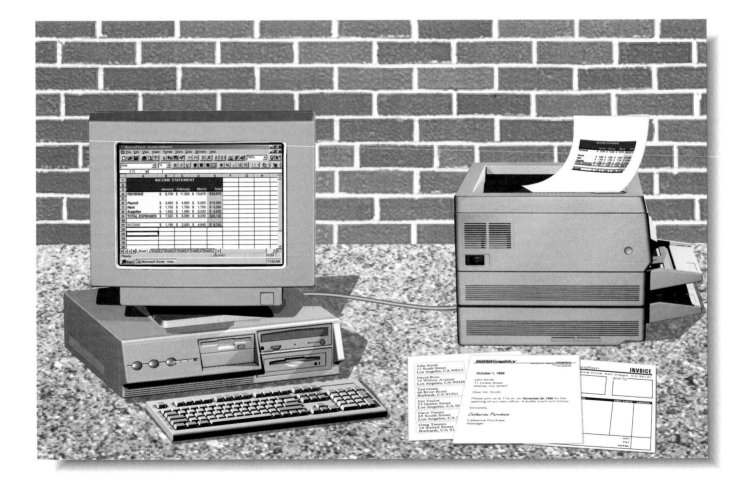

CHAPTER 2

Input and Output

What is a modem and why would you want one? What type of printer is best for you? This chapter will answer these questions and more.

A mouse is a handheld pointing device that lets you select and move items on your screen. A mouse can come in various shapes, colors and sizes.

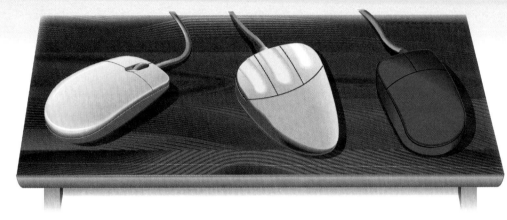

Most programs sold today are designed to work with a mouse. A mouse is essential when using Windows programs.

USE THE MOUSE

Resting your hand on the mouse, use your thumb and two rightmost fingers to move the mouse on the desk. Use your two remaining fingers to press the mouse buttons.

When you move the mouse on your desk, the pointer on the screen moves in the same direction. The pointer assumes different shapes (example: ▷ or I) depending on its location on the screen and the task you are performing.

MOUSE ACTIONS

There are four common
mouse actions.

Click

A click often selects an
item on the screen. To
click, press and release
the left mouse button.

Double-click

A double-click often opens
a document or starts a
program. To double-click,
quickly press and release
the left mouse button twice.

Drag and Drop

Dragging and dropping
makes it easy to move an
item on the screen. Position the pointer over
an item on the screen and then press and hold
down the left mouse button. Still holding down
the button, move the pointer to where you want
to place the item and then release the button.

Right-click

A right-click often
displays a list of
commands on the
screen. To right-click,
press and release the
right mouse button.

LEFT-HANDED USERS

If you are left-handed, you can
switch the functions of the left and
right mouse buttons to make the
mouse easier to use. For example,
to click an item, you would
press the right button instead
of the left.

WHEELED MOUSE

A wheeled mouse has a wheel between
the left and right mouse buttons.
You can often use this wheel to scroll
through information or zoom in and
out. The Microsoft IntelliMouse
is a popular example of
a wheeled mouse.

MOUSE

MOUSE PAD

A mouse pad provides a smooth surface for moving the mouse and can brighten up your desk. A mouse pad also reduces the amount of dirt that enters the mouse and protects your desk from scratches.

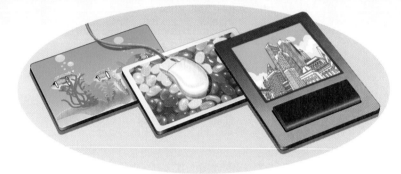

Hard plastic mouse pads tend to attract less dirt and provide a smoother surface than fabric-covered mouse pads.

You can buy mouse pads displaying interesting designs or pictures at most computer stores. Some mouse pads have built-in wrist support for increased comfort.

CLEAN THE MOUSE

You should occasionally remove and clean the ball inside the mouse. Make sure you also remove dust and dirt from the inside to help ensure smooth motion of the mouse.

CORDLESS MOUSE

A cordless mouse runs on a battery and reduces the clutter on your desk by eliminating the mouse cord. When you move the mouse on your desk, the mouse sends signals through the air to your computer, the same way a remote control sends signals to a television.

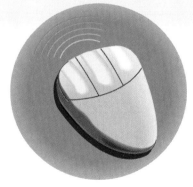

OTHER POINTING DEVICES

Joystick

A joystick helps you control the movement of people and objects in many computer games. Joysticks are used for arcade-type computer games because they let you move quickly and accurately in any direction.

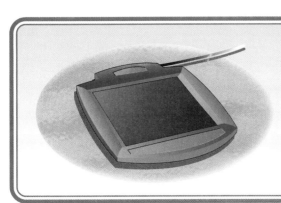

Touchpad

A touchpad is a surface that is sensitive to pressure and motion. When you move your fingertip across the pad, the pointer on the screen moves in the same direction.

Trackball

A trackball is an upside-down mouse that remains stationary on your desk. You roll the ball with your fingers or palm to move the pointer on the screen. A trackball is a great alternative to a mouse when you have limited desk space.

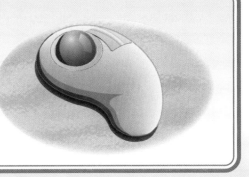

KEYBOARD

The keys on a keyboard let you enter information and instructions into a computer.

Most keyboards have 101 keys. Your keyboard may look different from the keyboard shown here.

Escape Key

You can press **Esc** to quit a task you are performing.

Caps Lock and Shift Keys

These keys let you enter text in uppercase (ABC) and lowercase (abc) letters.

Press **Caps Lock** to change the case of all letters you type. Press the key again to return to the original case.

Press **Shift** in combination with another key to type an uppercase letter.

Function Keys

These keys let you quickly perform specific tasks. For example, in many programs you can press **F1** to display help information.

Ctrl and Alt Keys

You can use the **Ctrl** or **Alt** key in combination with another key to perform a specific task. For example, in some programs you can press **Ctrl** and **S** to save a document.

Windows Key

You can press the **Windows** key to quickly display the Start menu when using the Windows 95, 98 or NT operating systems.

Spacebar

You can press the **Spacebar** to insert a blank space.

Backspace Key

You can press
Backspace to remove
the character to the
left of the cursor.

Delete Key

You can press
Delete to remove
the character to the
right of the cursor.

Status Lights

These lights indicate
whether the **Num Lock**
or **Caps Lock** features
are on or off.

Numeric Keypad

When the **Num Lock** light
is on, you can use the
number keys (0 through 9)
to enter numbers. When
the **Num Lock** light is off,
you can use these keys
to move the cursor
around the screen.
To turn the light
on or off, press
Num Lock.

Application Key

You can press the
Application key to
quickly display the
shortcut menu for an
item on your screen.

Enter Key

You can press **Enter** to tell
the computer to carry out
a task. In a word processing
program, press this key to
start a new paragraph.

Arrow Keys

These keys let you
move the cursor
around the screen.

KEYBOARD

Wireless

Wireless keyboards do not use a cable to connect to a computer. A wireless keyboard uses an infrared transmitter and receiver to communicate with a computer.

Ergonomic

Ergonomically designed keyboards position your hands naturally and support your wrists so you can work more comfortably.

Built-in Enhancements

Many new keyboards include built-in enhancements such as touchpads, microphones, speakers and volume controls.

CLEAN A KEYBOARD

Over time, dust and dirt can accumulate on a keyboard, causing the keys to stick or not respond when pressed. To remove dust and dirt, you can run a vacuum cleaner over the keys.

The plastic outer surface of the keyboard can be cleaned with a damp cloth. You should not attempt to open your keyboard to clean the inside, as this can damage the keyboard.

Typing Programs

There are programs available to help you improve your typing skills. You can buy these programs at most computer stores.

Position Your Hands

Most keyboards have small bumps on the **F** and **J** keys. These bumps help you position your fingers without looking at the keyboard.

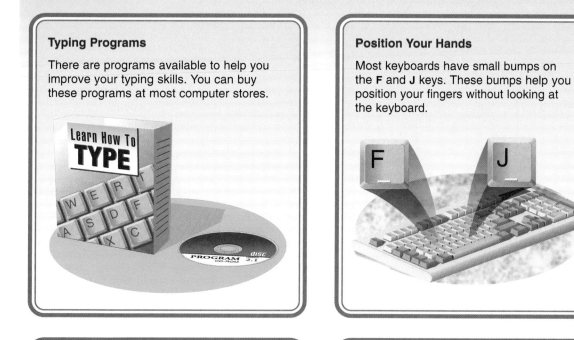

Special Characters

Many programs let you enter special characters or symbols that do not appear on the keyboard.

Keyboard Shortcuts

Most programs let you select commands by using keyboard shortcuts. These shortcuts are often shown on the menus. For example, to select the **Save** command in some programs, you can press the **Ctrl** and **S** keys.

A plus sign (+) between two key names tells you to press and hold down the first key before pressing the second key.

A printer produces a paper copy of the information displayed on the screen.

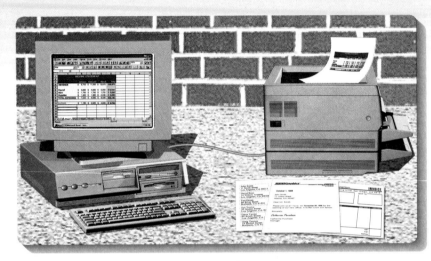

You can buy a printer that produces black-and-white or color images.

You can use a printer to produce letters, invoices, newsletters, transparencies, labels, packing slips and much more.

CHOOSE A PRINTER

There are several factors to consider when buying a printer.

■ Make sure the printer will work with your computer and software.

■ Check the size and type of paper the printer accepts. Some printers can print on large sheets of paper.

■ Check the cost of materials such as ink and paper.

■ Check the amount of paper the printer tray can hold.

■ If you want to print on envelopes, make sure the printer will accept envelopes.

PRINTER SPEED

The speed of a printer determines how quickly it can print the pages you selected. Speed is measured in pages per minute (ppm). A higher speed results in faster output.

A complicated page, such as a page that contains images, takes longer to print than a page that contains only text.

PRINTER RESOLUTION

The resolution of a printer determines the quality of the images it can produce. A higher resolution results in sharper, more detailed images.

Printer resolution is measured in dots per inch (dpi). Generally, a resolution of 600 dpi is acceptable for most office documents. 1200 dpi printers are better for printing images.

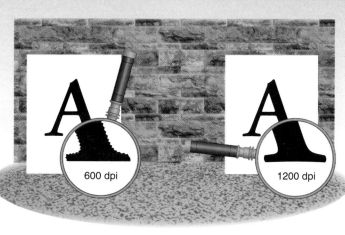

600 dpi

1200 dpi

A printed image consists of thousands of tiny dots. A high resolution printer produces clearer images because the images are made up of a larger number of smaller dots.

Resolution can also be expressed with two numbers (example: 600 x 600 dpi). These numbers describe the number of dots a printer can produce across and down in one square inch.

PRINTER

An ink-jet printer produces high-quality documents at a relatively low price. This type of printer is ideal for routine business and personal documents.

An ink-jet printer has a print head that sprays ink through small holes onto a page.

Speed

Most ink-jet printers produce images at a speed of 0.5 to 4 pages per minute (ppm).

Resolution

The resolution, or quality, of the images produced by an ink-jet printer ranges from 180 to 720 dots per inch (dpi).

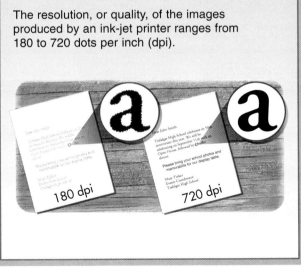

Ink

Ink-jet printers use ink stored in cartridges. When the ink runs out, you replace the cartridge.

Many ink cartridges have an expiry date on them. Before you buy a new cartridge, you should make sure it has not expired.

Paper

Ink-jet printers accept 8 ½ by 11-inch paper. Some ink-jet printers accept larger paper sizes. Ink-jet printers also accept envelopes, labels and transparencies. For best printing results, make sure you buy items designed specifically for use with ink-jet printers.

Color

Color ink-jet printers are very popular because they are less expensive than color laser printers and still produce high-quality color images.

A color ink-jet printer sprays cyan, magenta, yellow and black ink to create images on a page. Lower-cost color ink-jet printers create black by mixing the cyan, magenta and yellow ink. The best color images come from printers that offer black as a separate color.

Some ink-jet printers use more than four colors of ink, which allows you to print even higher-quality color images.

PRINTER

LASER PRINTER

A laser printer is a high-speed printer that is ideal for business and personal documents and for proofing professional graphics work.

A laser printer works like a photocopier to produce high-quality images on a page.

Speed

Most laser printers produce images at a speed of 4 to 20 pages per minute (ppm).

Resolution

The resolution, or quality, of the images produced by a laser printer ranges from 300 to 1200 dots per inch (dpi).

Memory

Laser printers store pages in built-in memory before printing. A typical laser printer comes with 4 MB to 8 MB of memory.

Memory is important for laser printers that produce images at high resolutions, such as 1200 dpi. Memory is also important for laser printers that print on large paper sizes and process complex print jobs.

Paper

All laser printers can print on 8 ½ by 11-inch paper, envelopes, labels and transparencies. For best printing results, make sure you buy items designed specifically for use with laser printers.

Toner

Like photocopiers, laser printers use a fine powdered ink, called toner, which comes in a cartridge. When the toner runs out, you buy a new cartridge.

Color

You can buy laser printers that produce color images. A color laser printer is more expensive than a color ink-jet printer, but it produces superior output.

FONT

A font is a set of characters with a particular design and size. You can use different fonts to make documents more attractive and interesting.

Most printers come with a few built-in fonts, called resident fonts. Documents created with resident fonts print faster than documents that use the fonts stored on your computer.

TrueType Font

A TrueType font generates characters using mathematical formulas. You can change the size of a TrueType font without distorting the font. A TrueType font will print exactly as it appears on the screen.

Bitmapped Font

A bitmapped font stores each character as a picture made up of a pattern of dots. If you change the size of a bitmapped font, the font may become distorted.

PRINT BUFFER AND SPOOLER

A computer can send data faster than a printer can accept and process the data. A print spooler or print buffer acts like a dam, holding the data and then releasing it at a speed the printer can handle.

Print Buffer

A print buffer is a section of memory in a printer that stores information you selected to print. When the buffer is full, the computer must wait before sending more data to the printer.

Print Spooler

A print spooler is a program on your computer that stores information you selected to print.

A print spooler can store more information than a print buffer and lets you continue using your computer without having to wait for a document to finish printing. Windows comes with a built-in print spooler.

MONITOR AND VIDEO CARD

The monitor and video card work together to display text and images on the screen.

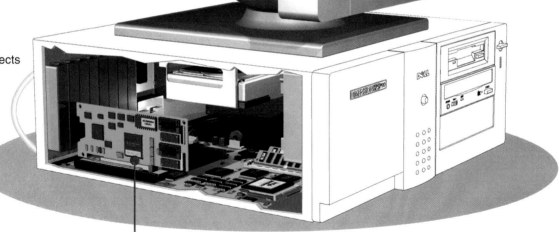

Monitor

A monitor displays text and images generated by the video card.

Screen

The screen is the display area of a monitor.

A cable connects the monitor to the video card in the computer.

Video Card

The video card is a circuit board that plugs into an expansion slot inside the computer. The video card translates instructions from the computer to a form the monitor can understand.

A video card is also called a video adapter, video board, graphics adapter, graphics board or graphics card.

Size

The size of a monitor is measured diagonally across the screen. Common monitor sizes are 14, 15, 17 and 21 inches. Larger monitors are more expensive and are ideal for desktop publishing and working with images or large spreadsheets.

Manufacturers usually advertise the diagonal measurement of the picture tube inside the monitor, which is greater than the actual viewing area. Make sure you ask for the size of the viewing area.

Flat-panel

A flat-panel monitor uses Liquid Crystal Display (LCD), which is the same type of display found in most digital wristwatches. In the past, flat-panel screens were only used on portable computers, but now full-size flat-panel monitors are available for desktop computers.

Flat-panel monitors are more expensive than desktop monitors, but are lighter, take up less desk space and use less electricity.

Dot Pitch

The dot pitch is the distance between tiny dots on a screen. The dot pitch determines the sharpness of images on the screen.

The smaller the dot pitch, the crisper the images. Select a monitor with a dot pitch of 0.28 mm or less.

MONITOR AND VIDEO CARD

Refresh Rate

The refresh rate determines the speed that a monitor redraws, or updates, images. The higher the refresh rate, the less flicker on the screen. This helps reduce eye strain.

The refresh rate is measured in hertz (Hz) and tells you the number of times per second the monitor redraws the entire screen. A monitor with a refresh rate of 72 Hz or more is recommended.

Controls

Monitors have controls to adjust the brightness, contrast and other features of the images displayed on the screen. You can find controls on the screen or on the monitor.

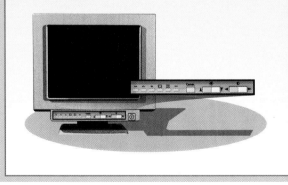

Tilt-and-swivel Base

A tilt-and-swivel base lets you adjust the angle of the screen. This lets you reduce the glare from overhead lighting and view the screen more comfortably.

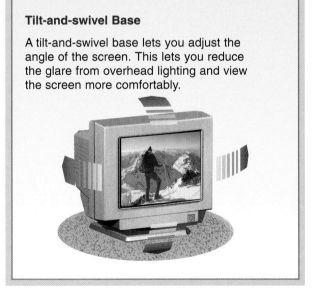

Electromagnetic Radiation

Any device that uses electricity produces ElectroMagnetic Radiation (EMR). You can protect yourself from potentially harmful effects by remaining a safe distance away from electrical devices.

Monitors emit EMR, but you can minimize the risk by buying a monitor that meets MPR II guidelines. The MPR II guidelines define acceptable levels of EMR.

You can further minimize the risk by turning off the monitor when it is not in use. Also avoid sitting near the sides or back of a monitor, which emit more EMR than the front.

Energy Star

The Environmental Protection Agency (EPA) developed an energy-saving guideline called ENERGY STAR to reduce wasted energy and the pollution it causes.

When you do not use an ENERGY STAR computer for a period of time, the monitor and computer enter an energy-saving sleep mode. You awaken the computer by moving the mouse or pressing a key on the keyboard.

MONITOR AND VIDEO CARD

Screen Saver

A screen saver is a moving picture or pattern that appears on the screen when you do not use a computer for a period of time.

Screen savers were originally designed to prevent screen burn, which occurs when an image appears in a fixed position for a period of time.

Today's monitors are designed to prevent screen burn, but people still use screen savers for entertainment.

Windows provides several screen savers. You can purchase more sophisticated screen savers at most computer stores.

Using a process called Webcasting, you can also use screen savers that display customized, up-to-the-minute information. This information is transferred to your computer from the Internet.

Glare Filter

A glare filter fits over the front of a monitor to reduce the amount of light reflected off the computer screen. This helps reduce eye strain.

Most glare filters also help block the radiation coming from the front of the monitor.

VIDEO CARD MEMORY

A video card has memory chips. These chips store the information that is displayed on the screen.

Most computers require at least 2 MB of video card memory.

VRAM

Video Random Access Memory (VRAM) is a type of memory specifically designed for video cards. VRAM is ideal for displaying complex images.

Extended Data Out Dynamic RAM (EDO DRAM) and Window RAM (WRAM) are two other types of video card memory.

AGP

An Accelerated Graphics Port (AGP) video card uses an AGP bus to communicate directly with your computer's main memory. This allows you to quickly display complex images on your monitor.

AGP is specially designed to meet the high demands of displaying 3-D images.

MONITOR AND VIDEO CARD

Resolution determines the amount of information a monitor can display.

Resolution is measured by the number of horizontal and vertical pixels. A pixel is the smallest element on the screen. Pixel is short for picture element.

A multisync monitor lets you adjust the resolution to suit your needs. Other monitors can display only one resolution.

| 640 x 480 | 800 x 600 | 1,024 x 768 | 1,280 x 1,024 |

Lower resolutions display larger images so you can see information more clearly.

Higher resolutions display smaller images so you can display more information at once.

COLOR DEPTH

The number of colors a monitor can display determines how realistic images appear on a screen. More colors result in more realistic images.

VGA

Video Graphics Array (VGA) monitors display 16 colors at a resolution of 640 x 480. This is the minimum standard for computer systems.

SVGA

Super Video Graphics Array (SVGA) monitors display more colors and higher resolutions than VGA monitors. Most new computer systems offer SVGA.

16 Colors (4-bit color)

Choppy-looking images.

256 Colors (8-bit color)

Ideal for most home, business and game applications.

**65,536 Colors
(16-bit color)**

Ideal for video and desktop publishing applications. Unless you are a trained professional, it is difficult to distinguish between 16-bit and 24-bit color.

**16,777,216 Colors
(24-bit color)**

Ideal for photographic work. This setting is also called true color because it displays more colors than the human eye can distinguish.

TV TUNER CARD

A TV tuner card allows you to watch television programs on your computer.

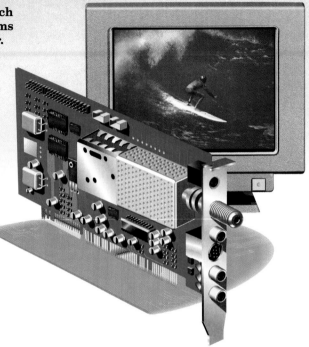

A TV tuner card is a circuit board that plugs into an expansion slot in the computer.

TV tuner cards combine computer and television technology. This combination, or convergence, of technologies is creating an exciting new form of entertainment and communication.

Video Card

TV tuner cards require a video card to operate. Most TV tuner cards connect to the video card in your computer, but some TV tuner cards have a built-in video card.

TV TUNER CARD FEATURES

Resize

TV tuner cards can display a television program using the entire display area of a monitor or using a window that you can easily resize to suit your needs. This is useful if you want to watch a television program while performing other tasks on your computer.

Closed Captioning

Most TV tuner cards can scan the closed captioning text of a television channel for a keyword you specify. When the keyword appears, the TV tuner card displays the television program on your monitor. Most TV tuner cards also allow you to save the closed captioning text from a television program as a file on your hard drive.

Intercast Technology

Some television channels use Intercast technology to broadcast additional information with their programs. This allows you to watch a television program and view text and images related to the program at the same time.

For example, when you watch a car race, you can also view information such as the average speed of a driver. Most TV tuner cards support Intercast technology.

Video Capture

Most TV tuner cards allow you to save still images and full-motion video clips from a television program as a file on your hard drive. You can then use these images and video clips in documents, e-mail messages or presentations.

MODEM

A modem lets computers exchange information through telephone lines.

A modem translates computer information into a form that can transmit over phone lines.

Phone Line

You do not need a separate phone line to use a modem. You can use the same phone line for telephone and modem calls. If your telephone and modem share the same line, make sure you turn off the call waiting feature when using your modem, since this feature could disrupt the modem connection.

The receiving modem translates the information it receives into a form the computer can understand.

MODEM APPLICATIONS

Connect to the Internet

A modem lets you connect to the Internet and online services such as America Online and AT&T WorldNet. This lets you access a vast amount of information and meet thousands of people with similar interests.

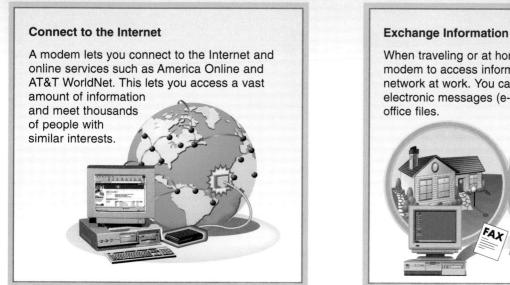

Exchange Information

When traveling or at home, you can use a modem to access information stored on the network at work. You can send and receive electronic messages (e-mail) and work with office files.

Send and Receive Faxes

Most modems can send and receive faxes. With a fax modem, you can create a document on your computer and then fax the document to another computer or fax machine.

When a computer receives a fax, the document appears on the screen. You can review and print the document, but you cannot edit the document unless you have Optical Character Recognition (OCR) software.

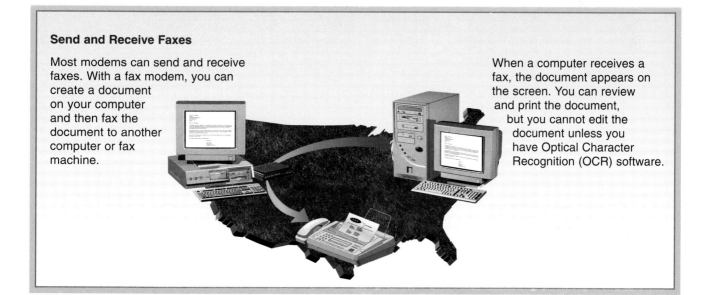

MODEM

Internal Modem

An internal modem is a circuit board that plugs into an expansion slot in a computer. This type of modem is generally less expensive than an external modem, but is more difficult to set up.

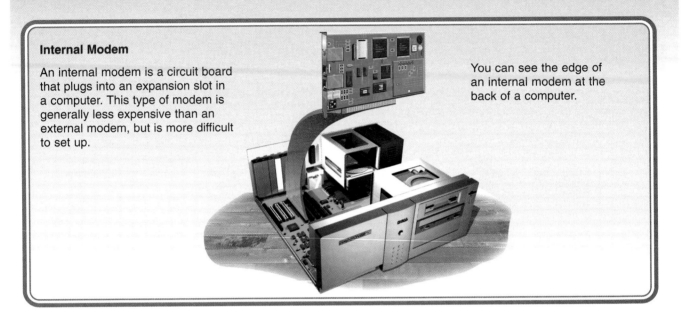

You can see the edge of an internal modem at the back of a computer.

External Modem

An external modem is a small box that plugs into the back of a computer. An external modem takes up room on your desk, but you can use this type of modem with more than one computer.

If you are using an external modem with an older computer, make sure the computer uses a 16550 UART chip. This will ensure that the computer can handle current modem speeds. A UART chip controls the flow of information to and from the modem.

Status lights on the modem tell you about the current transmission. For example, the RD light is on when the modem is receiving data.

MODEM SPEED

The speed of a modem determines how fast it can send and receive information through telephone lines.

Modem speed is measured in bits per second (bps). You should buy a modem with a speed of at least 33,600 bps.

Modem speeds of 56,000 bps are now available.

Modem speed is also measured in kilobits per second (Kbps). For example, a 33,600 bps modem is also referred to as a 33.6 Kbps modem.

Buy the fastest modem you can afford. Faster modems transfer information more quickly. This will save you time and reduce online service charges and long distance charges.

Line Quality

The speed at which information transfers depends on the quality of the phone line. For example, a modem with a speed of 33,600 bps may not reach that speed if the phone line quality is poor.

Modem Standards

Modem standards ensure that modems made by different manufacturers can communicate with each other. V.90 is the new standard for 56 Kbps modems. A V.90 modem can receive data at a speed of 56 Kbps, but can only send data at a speed of 33.6 Kbps.

MODEM

██ HOW MODEMS COMMUNICATE

Communications Program

A modem needs a communications program to manage the transmission of information with another modem. This type of program usually comes packaged with a modem.

Handshake

Before exchanging information, modems perform a handshake just as two people shake hands to greet each other. A handshake establishes how the modems will exchange information.

Modems must use the same speed when exchanging information. A fast modem can talk to a slower modem, but they will communicate at the slower speed. You may find that some online services use lower speed modems.

Online

You are online when your modem has successfully connected to another modem. This means the modems are ready and able to exchange information. When your modem is not connected to another modem, you are offline.

DATA COMPRESSION

A modem can compress, or squeeze together, data sent to another modem to speed the transfer of data. The speed of data transfer depends on the type of file being sent. For example, a text file will compress significantly more than an image file.

When the information reaches its intended destination, the receiving modem decompresses the information.

ERROR CONTROL

A modem uses error control to ensure that information reliably reaches its destination.

When you send information using a modem, the information is broken down into smaller pieces, called packets. When the packets arrive at the intended destination, the receiving modem checks for damaged packets. If a packet is damaged, the modem that sent the information is asked to send a new copy.

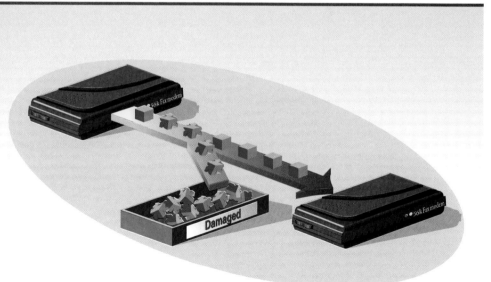

MODEM

ISDN

Instead of connecting to the Internet using a modem with a regular telephone line, you can use an Integrated Services Digital Network (ISDN) line. People working at home who want fast access to information at the office often use an ISDN line. Many companies also use an ISDN line to connect several networked computers to the Internet.

ISDN transfers information between the Internet service provider and your home several times faster than a modem.

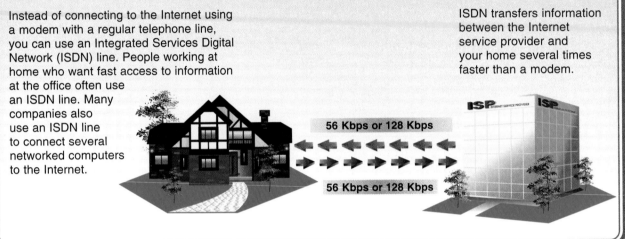

56 Kbps or 128 Kbps

56 Kbps or 128 Kbps

Cable Modem

A cable modem lets you connect to the Internet with the same cable that attaches to a television set. Many cable companies offer cable modems and cable Internet services. Contact your local cable company for more information.

A cable modem can transfer information from the Internet service provider to your home hundreds of times faster than a modem.

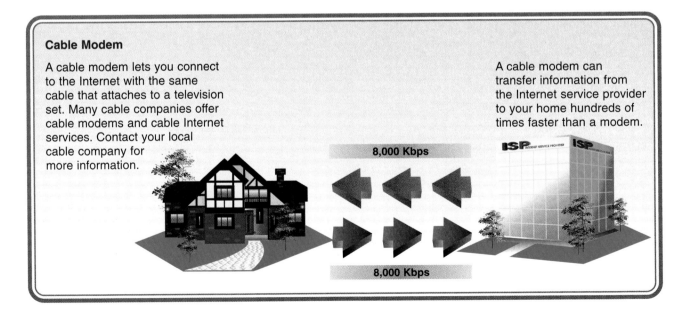

8,000 Kbps

8,000 Kbps

ADSL

Asymmetric Digital Subscriber Line (ADSL) is a high-speed connection to the Internet that uses regular telephone lines. Some telephone companies offer ADSL services.

ADSL can send information to your home hundreds of times faster than a modem, but returns information back to the Internet service provider at a much slower speed.

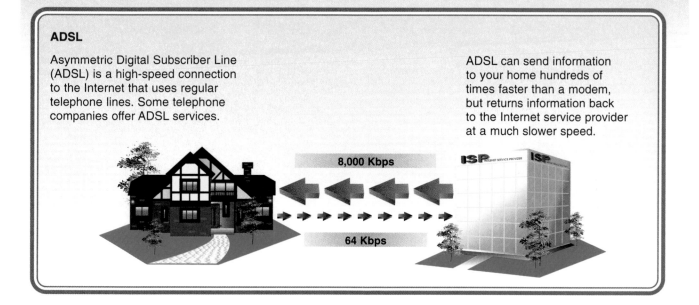

Direct-broadcast Satellite

The satellite companies that transmit information such as HBO and CNN to your television set also offer access to the Internet.

Satellites are often the best choice for people who want a high-speed connection to the Internet, but live in rural areas where other modem alternatives are not available.

Satellites can send information to your home many times faster than a modem. You need a standard 33.6 Kbps modem to send information back to the Internet service provider.

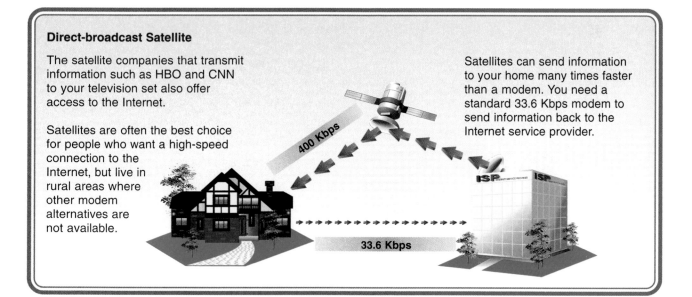

SOUND CARD

A sound card lets a computer play and record high-quality sound.

A sound card is a circuit board that plugs into an expansion slot in the computer.

A sound card is also called a sound board or audio card.

Speakers

You need speakers to hear the sound generated by a sound card. You should buy speakers with a built-in amplifier to strengthen the sound signal and improve the performance.

SOUND CARD APPLICATIONS

Games and Multimedia Presentations

A sound card lets you hear music, speech and sound effects during games and multimedia presentations.

Record Sounds

You can use a sound card to record music, speech and sound effects. You can then add the sounds to documents and presentations. You can also use a sound card to compose music on your computer.

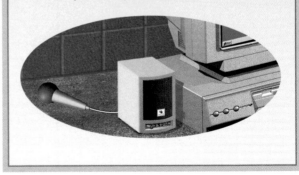

SOUND CARD CONNECTIONS

You can see the edge of a sound card at the back of a computer. A sound card has a port and several jacks where you can plug in external devices.

The edge of your sound card may look different from the sound card shown here.

Joystick

This port lets you connect a joystick or a MIDI device such as a music keyboard.

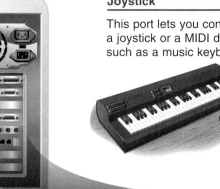

Line In

This jack lets you connect a cassette or CD player to play music.

Spk Out

This jack lets you connect speakers or headphones to hear sound generated by a sound card.

Line Out

This jack lets you connect an amplifier to play sound through your home stereo.

Mic In

This jack lets you connect a microphone to record speech and other sounds.

SOUND CARD

CHOOSE A SOUND CARD

Sampling Size and Rate

The sampling size and rate of a sound card determines the quality of the sound produced.

For good sound quality, buy a sound card with a 16-bit sampling size and a 44.1 KHz sampling rate.

If possible, listen to the sounds produced by various sound cards before making your purchase.

Sound Blaster

Make sure you buy a Sound Blaster compatible sound card to ensure your computer has full sound capabilities.

Full-duplex

A full-duplex sound card lets you talk and listen at the same time. When using a computer to have a conversation over the Internet, a full-duplex sound card lets people talk at the same time. With a half-duplex card, people must take turns talking.

MIDI

Musical Instrument Digital Interface (MIDI) is a set of instructions that allow computers and musical devices to exchange data. This lets you use a computer to play, record and edit music. Many musicians use MIDI to compose music on a computer.

A sound card that supports MIDI ensures that a computer can generate the sounds often found in games, CD-ROM titles and presentation packages.

There are two ways a sound card can produce MIDI sound.

FM Synthesis

FM synthesis imitates the sounds of musical instruments and speech. This results in less realistic sound. FM synthesis is found on low to mid-range sound cards.

Wavetable Synthesis

Wavetable synthesis uses actual recordings of musical instruments and speech. This results in rich, realistic sound. Wavetable synthesis is found on high-quality sound cards.

A scanner is a device that reads images and text into a computer.

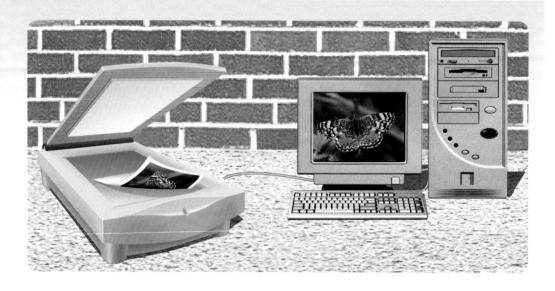

Scan Images

You can scan images such as photographs, drawings and logos into a computer. You can then use the images in documents, such as reports or newsletters.

Most scanners come with image editing software, which lets you change the appearance of a scanned image.

Scan Text

You can scan text to quickly enter documents into a computer. This lets you scan interesting paper documents and e-mail them to friends or colleagues. You can also scan office documents to store them on your computer for quick access.

Most scanners come with Optical Character Recognition (OCR) software. This software places scanned text into a document that can be edited in a word processor.

TYPES OF SCANNERS

Handheld Scanner

A handheld scanner is the least expensive type of scanner. A handheld scanner has a scanning width of approximately four inches and is ideal for copying small images, such as signatures, logos and small photographs.

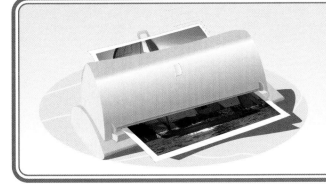

Sheet-fed Scanner

A sheet-fed scanner produces more reliable scans than a handheld scanner and is less expensive and more compact than a flatbed scanner. A sheet-fed scanner can scan only single sheets of paper. If you want to scan a page from a book, you have to tear out the page.

Flatbed Scanner

A flatbed scanner is the most versatile type of scanner. A flatbed scanner is ideal when you want to scan pages from a book without tearing out the pages.

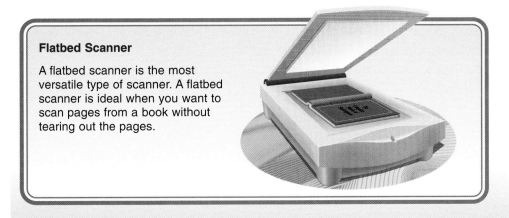

COLOR

Grayscale Scanner

A grayscale scanner reads images using black, white and shades of gray. A grayscale scanner is ideal for scanning text or when you plan to print scanned images on a black-and-white printer.

Color Scanner

A color scanner is more expensive than a grayscale scanner and reads images using shades of red, blue and green. A color scanner is ideal for scanning images you plan to display in color, such as photographs and illustrations.

Choose the Scanning Mode

When scanning an image, you can choose the scanning mode.

Line Art

The line art mode scans an image using black and white.

Grayscale

The grayscale mode scans an image using black, white and shades of gray.

Color

The color mode scans an image using shades of red, blue and green.

RESOLUTION

The resolution of a scanner determines the amount of detail the scanner can detect.

Scanner resolution is measured in dots per inch (dpi). Some scanners can detect up to 2400 dpi.

Choose the Resolution

Scanning an image at a high resolution results in a clearer, more detailed image, but requires more scanning time and storage space.

You usually do not need to scan an image at a higher resolution than a printer can produce or a monitor can display.

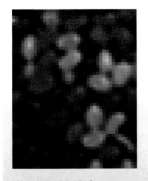

20 dpi

72 dpi

300 dpi

If you plan to print an image on a 300 dpi printer, you do not need to scan at a resolution higher than 300 dpi. Monitors have a maximum resolution of 72 dpi. If you plan to display an image on a monitor or on the Internet, you do not need to scan at a resolution higher than 72 dpi.

DIGITAL CAMERA

A digital camera lets you take photos and use them on your computer.

You can place the photos in documents, on a Web page or in e-mail messages to share them with your friends and relatives.

PROGRAMS

Most digital cameras come with a program called an image editor. Image editors allow you to view and edit photos on your computer. For example, you can change the colors or add and remove objects in your photos. Popular image editors include Adobe Systems PhotoDeluxe and Microsoft Picture It!

FEATURES

Many digital cameras come with a color Liquid Crystal Display (LCD) screen, which is the same type of display found in notebook computers. You can use the LCD screen to preview your shots and view photos you have taken.

A digital camera may also include a built-in flash or a zoom lens. Some digital cameras include a feature that lets you connect the camera to a TV so you can view your pictures on the screen.

RESOLUTION

The resolution of a digital camera determines the quality of photos the camera can produce.

The higher the resolution, the clearer and more detailed the photos. A digital camera with a resolution of 640 x 480 can produce photos suitable for viewing on a monitor. Digital cameras with a resolution of 1,152 x 864 or higher, called megapixel cameras, are best if you want to print good quality photos.

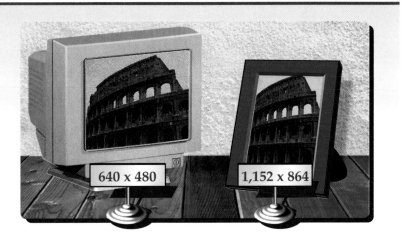

640 x 480

1,152 x 864

MEMORY

Digital cameras store photos in memory until you transfer the photos to your computer. Most digital cameras have either built-in or removable memory.

Built-in

The built-in memory in most digital cameras can store at least 20 photos. Once the built-in memory is full, you must transfer the photos to your computer before taking more photos.

Removable

Most digital cameras with removable memory store photos on a memory card. Some digital cameras store photos on a regular 3.5 inch floppy disk that fits inside the camera. You can replace a memory card or floppy disk when it is full.

CHAPTER 3

Processing

Wondering how a computer operates and processes information? Find out in this chapter.

MEMORY

Memory, also called Random Access Memory (RAM), temporarily stores data inside a computer.

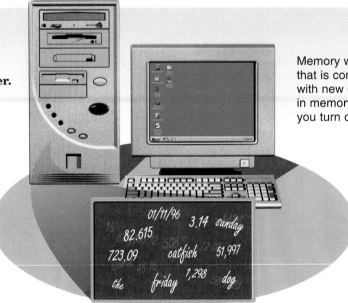

Memory works like a blackboard that is constantly overwritten with new data. The data stored in memory disappears when you turn off the computer.

MEMORY SIZE

The amount of memory determines the number of programs a computer can run at once and how fast programs will operate.

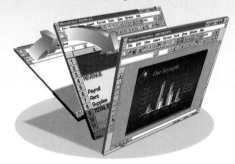

Memory is measured in bytes. You should buy a computer with at least 32 MB of memory, but 64 MB is recommended.

You can improve the performance of a computer by adding more memory.

PROGRAM REQUIREMENTS

A program will usually tell you the minimum amount of memory your computer needs to use the program.

System Requirements
- Pentium 90 MHz or higher
- Windows 95 or higher
- Memory: 16 MB
- Minimum install: 30 MB
- Monitor: VGA or above
- Mouse or other pointing device

WORD PROCESSOR
V 5.0
Create Professional Documents

MEMORY CHIPS

Dynamic RAM (DRAM) is a type of memory chip that makes up the main memory in many computer systems.

Synchronous DRAM (SDRAM) is a faster type of memory chip found in most new computer systems. Many new computers can use both DRAM and SDRAM memory chips.

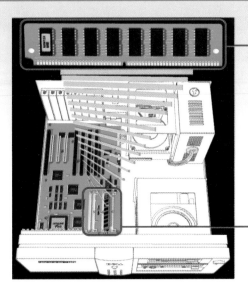

Memory Module

A memory module is a circuit board that holds memory chips. A Single In-line Memory Module (SIMM) holds up to nine memory chips. New computers also accept Dual In-line Memory Modules (DIMMs), which can hold up to 18 memory chips. You can add more memory to a computer by inserting additional memory modules.

Memory Module Socket

A memory module socket is a socket on the motherboard where you plug in a memory module.

VIRTUAL MEMORY

If you have limited memory or you have many programs open, your computer may need to use part of the hard drive to simulate more memory.

This simulated memory is called virtual memory and allows the computer to continue operating, but at a much slower speed.

ROM

Unlike RAM, Read-Only Memory (ROM) is permanent and cannot be changed. ROM stores instructions that help prepare the computer for use each time you turn on the computer.

The Central Processing Unit (CPU) is the main chip in a computer.

The CPU processes instructions, performs calculations and manages the flow of information through a computer system. The CPU performs millions of calculations every second.

The CPU is also called the microprocessor or processor.

CPU Complexity

Imagine a U.S. road map printed on a fingernail and you can imagine the complexity of a CPU. The elements in a CPU can be as small as 0.18 microns wide. By comparison, a human hair is about 100 microns wide.

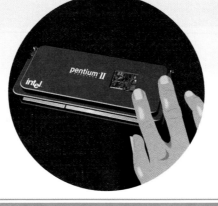

The manufacturing plants that produce CPUs are tens of thousands of times cleaner than hospital operating rooms. Ultra-sensitive dust filtering systems are needed to eliminate particles that could damage the CPUs.

CHOOSE A CPU

There are several factors that determine the performance of a CPU.

Manufacturer

The most popular CPUs for personal computers are made by Intel. Other companies that make CPUs include AMD and Cyrix.

Generation

Each new generation of CPUs is more powerful than the one before. Newer CPUs can process more instructions at a time.

CPU generations include the new Pentium II and the Pentium. The older 486 generation is obsolete.

When buying a new computer, do not consider anything less powerful than a Pentium II.

Speed

Each CPU generation is available in several speeds. The CPU speed is a major factor in determining how fast a computer operates. The faster the speed, the faster the computer operates.

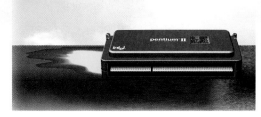

The speed of a CPU is measured in megahertz (MHz), or millions of cycles per second.

TYPES OF CPUs

Pentium

Intel's Pentium chip is ideal for computers using Windows 3.1, 95 and 98. The most common speeds for Pentium chips include 90, 133, 166 and 200 MHz.

Comparable CPU chips include Cyrix's 6x86 and MediaGX chips, as well as AMD's AMD-K5 chip.

MMX

Many Pentium chips with speeds of 166 MHz and higher support multimedia extensions, referred to as MMX. MMX dramatically improves the performance of multimedia tasks, such as the processing of graphics, video and sound. Intel is working on a new version of MMX, currently named Katmai.

Pentium II

Intel's Pentium II chip is the fastest CPU chip available and is ideal for computers using Windows 98 and NT. All Pentium II chips support MMX technology for improved multimedia performance.

Pentium II chips can have speeds of 233, 266, 300, 333, 350, 400, 450 and 500 MHz.

Comparable CPU chips include Cyrix's 6x86MX and M II chips, as well as AMD's AMD-K6 chip. These chips also support MMX technology.

Celeron

The Celeron chip is a fast and inexpensive CPU chip made by Intel. Celeron chips are based on Pentium II chips, but have less built-in memory. The Celeron chip is designed to meet the needs and budgets of most home computer users.

Celeron chips are available with speeds of 266, 300 and 333 MHz.

Pentium Pro

Intel's Pentium Pro chip is ideal for computers that use powerful operating systems, such as Windows NT and UNIX. Pentium Pro chips are available with speeds of 150, 166, 180 and 200 MHz.

The successor to the Pentium Pro chip is called the Pentium II Xeon.

Future CPUs

Intel's next generation of CPUs is expected to go well beyond the speed of the current Pentium II chips. This new CPU generation, currently named Merced, is being designed primarily for use in powerful network computers.

MEMORY CACHE

Memory cache speeds up the computer by storing data the computer has recently used.

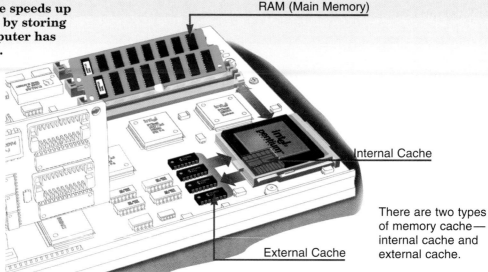

RAM (Main Memory)

Internal Cache

External Cache

There are two types of memory cache—internal cache and external cache.

INTERNAL CACHE

When the computer needs data, the computer first looks in the internal cache. Internal cache is on the CPU chip and provides the fastest way for the computer to get data. Internal cache is also called L1 or primary cache.

EXTERNAL CACHE

If the computer cannot find the data it needs in the internal cache, the computer looks in the external cache. External cache is usually on the motherboard and consists of Static RAM (SRAM) chips. External cache is also called L2 or secondary cache.

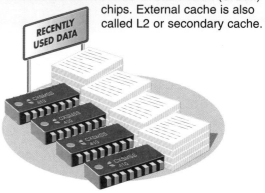

Accessing external cache is generally slower than internal cache. In Pentium II and Pentium Pro chips, the external cache is built into the CPU chip, which makes accessing the cache much faster.

RAM

If the computer cannot find the data it needs in the internal or external cache, the computer must get the data from the slower main memory, called RAM.

Each time the computer requests data from RAM, the computer places a copy of the data in the memory cache. This process constantly updates the memory cache so it always contains the most recently used data.

USING MEMORY CACHE

Using memory cache is similar to working with documents in your office. When you need information, you look for information in a specific order. Each step along the way takes up more of your valuable time.

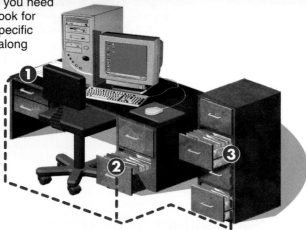

1 Look through documents on your desk (internal cache).

2 Look through documents in your desk drawer (external cache).

3 Look through documents in your filing cabinet (RAM).

Working without memory cache would be similar to looking through the filing cabinet each time you need a document.

The bus is the electronic pathway in a computer that carries information between devices.

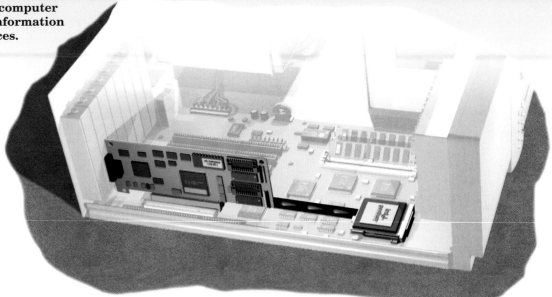

Bus Width

The bus width is similar to the number of lanes on a highway. The greater the width, the more data can flow along the bus at a time. Bus width is measured in bits. Eight bits equals one character.

Bus Speed

The bus speed is similar to the speed limit on a highway. The higher the speed, the faster data travels along the bus. Bus speed is measured in megahertz (MHz), or millions of cycles per second.

TYPES OF BUSES

ISA Bus

The Industry Standard Architecture (ISA) bus is the slowest and oldest type of bus. This bus is often used for transferring information to and from a slow device, such as a modem. The ISA bus has a width of 16 bits and a speed of 8 MHz.

The ISA bus is found in Pentium and Pentium II computers.

PCI Bus

The Peripheral Component Interconnect (PCI) bus is a sophisticated type of bus found in most new computers. This bus can handle many high-speed devices. The PCI bus can have a width of 32 or 64 bits and speeds of up to 100 MHz.

The PCI bus supports Plug and Play, which lets you add new devices to a computer without complex installation procedures.

The PCI bus is found in Pentium and Pentium II computers.

AGP Bus

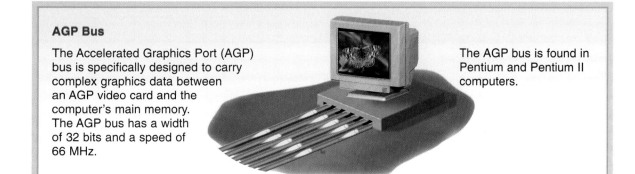

The Accelerated Graphics Port (AGP) bus is specifically designed to carry complex graphics data between an AGP video card and the computer's main memory. The AGP bus has a width of 32 bits and a speed of 66 MHz.

The AGP bus is found in Pentium and Pentium II computers.

CHAPTER 4

Storage Devices

What is a hard drive? What does a DVD-ROM drive do? Learn about storage devices in this chapter.

The hard drive is the primary device that a computer uses to store information.

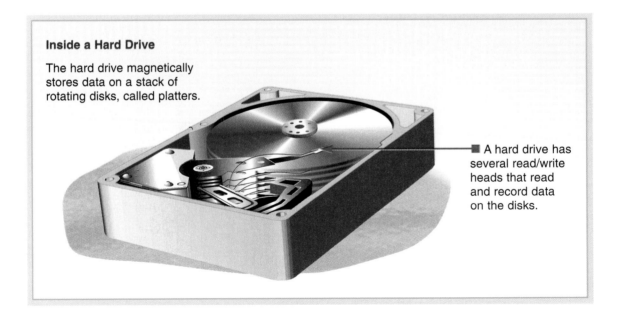

■ Most computers have one hard drive, located inside the computer case. If a computer has one hard drive, it is called drive C. If a computer has additional hard drives, they are called drives D, E, F, and so on.

The hard drive is also called the hard disk, hard disk drive or fixed disk drive.

■ The hard drive light is on when the computer is using the hard drive. Do not move the computer when this light is on.

Inside a Hard Drive

The hard drive magnetically stores data on a stack of rotating disks, called platters.

■ A hard drive has several read/write heads that read and record data on the disks.

HARD DRIVE CONTENTS

Program Files

A hard drive stores your programs.
When you buy a new program, you
must install, or copy, the program
files to your hard drive before you
can use the program.

Programs
come on a
CD-ROM disc,
DVD-ROM disc or
several floppy disks.

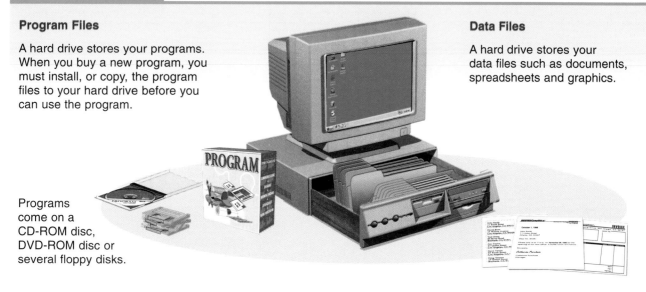

Data Files

A hard drive stores your
data files such as documents,
spreadsheets and graphics.

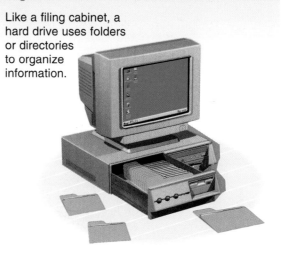

STORE FILES

Save Files

When you are creating a document, the
computer stores the document in temporary
memory. If you want to store a document for
future use, you must save the document to
the hard drive. If
you do not save
the document, the
document will be
lost when there is
a power failure or
you turn off the
computer.

Organize Files

Like a filing cabinet, a
hard drive uses folders
or directories
to organize
information.

 HARD DRIVE

Capacity

The amount of information a hard drive can store is measured in bytes.

A hard drive with a capacity of 3 to 4 GB will suit most home and business users.

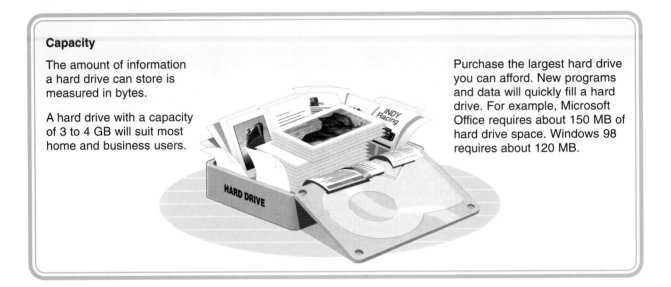

Purchase the largest hard drive you can afford. New programs and data will quickly fill a hard drive. For example, Microsoft Office requires about 150 MB of hard drive space. Windows 98 requires about 120 MB.

Speed

The speed at which the rotating disks in the hard drive, called platters, spin is measured in Revolutions Per Minute (RPM). The higher the RPM, the faster the hard drive can find and record data on the platters.

The speed at which a hard drive finds data is referred to as the average access time. Average access time is measured in milliseconds (ms). One millisecond equals 1/1000 of a second. Most hard drives have an average access time of 8 to 15 ms. The lower the average access time, the faster the hard drive.

EIDE

Enhanced Integrated Drive Electronics (EIDE) is a fast way to connect a hard drive and other devices to a computer. All new computers come with an EIDE connection. EIDE is often referred to as IDE.

EIDE can support a total of four devices, including hard drives, CD-ROM drives, DVD-ROM drives and tape drives.

Ultra Direct Memory Access (UDMA) is an enhancement to EIDE that increases the speed at which data transfers over an EIDE connection.

SCSI

Small Computer System Interface (SCSI, pronounced "scuzzy") is the fastest, most flexible, but most expensive way to connect a hard drive and other devices to a computer.

The most common type of SCSI can connect up to seven devices, including removable drives, CD-ROM drives, DVD-ROM drives, tape drives and scanners.

There are other types of SCSI available that can transmit data faster and connect more devices.

DISK CACHE

The disk cache speeds up the computer by storing data the computer has recently used.

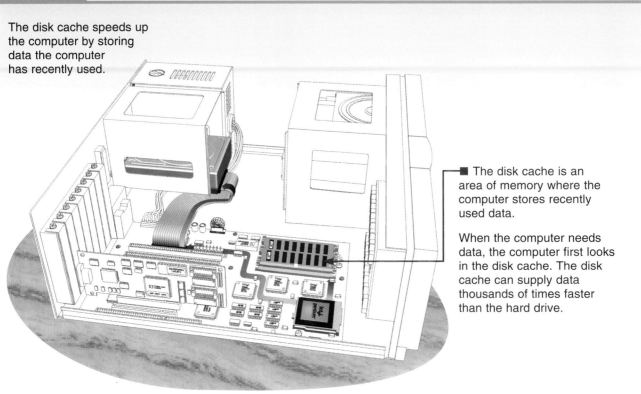

■ The disk cache is an area of memory where the computer stores recently used data.

When the computer needs data, the computer first looks in the disk cache. The disk cache can supply data thousands of times faster than the hard drive.

If the computer cannot find the data it needs in the disk cache, the computer looks on the hard drive.

Each time the computer requests data from the hard drive, the computer places a copy of the data in the disk cache. This process constantly updates the disk cache so it always contains the most recently used data.

HARD DRIVE

DISK CACHE

Virus

A virus is a program that disrupts the normal operation of a computer. A virus can cause a variety of problems, such as the appearance of annoying messages on the screen or the destruction of information on the hard drive.

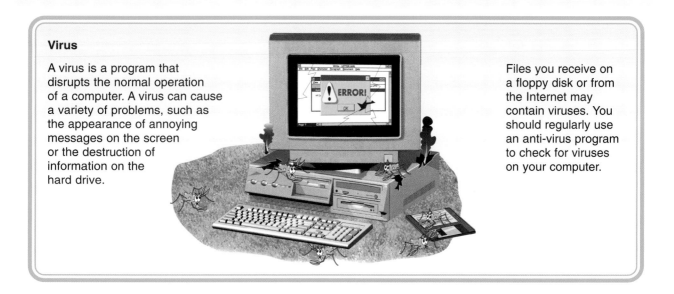

Files you receive on a floppy disk or from the Internet may contain viruses. You should regularly use an anti-virus program to check for viruses on your computer.

Back Up Data

You should copy the files stored on your hard drive to removable disks or tape cartridges. This provides extra copies in case the original files are stolen or damaged due to viruses or computer failure. Most operating systems come with a backup program.

You only need to back up your own work. You do not need to back up programs stored on your computer since you can use the original program disks to re-install the programs.

HARD DRIVE

Defragment a Drive

A fragmented hard drive stores parts of a file in many different locations. To retrieve a file, the computer must search many areas of the drive.

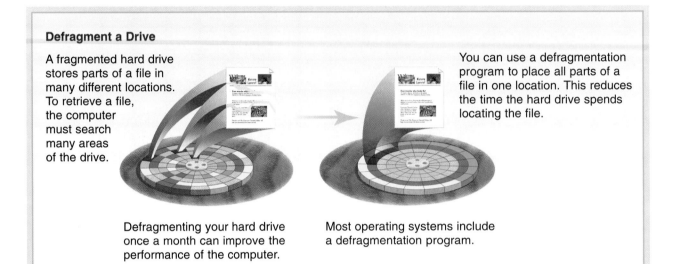

You can use a defragmentation program to place all parts of a file in one location. This reduces the time the hard drive spends locating the file.

Defragmenting your hard drive once a month can improve the performance of the computer.

Most operating systems include a defragmentation program.

Repair a Drive

You can improve the performance of a computer by using a disk repair program to search for and repair disk errors. You should check a hard drive for errors at least once a month.

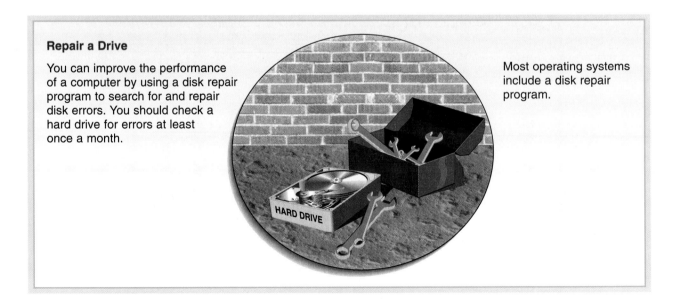

Most operating systems include a disk repair program.

CREATE MORE DISK SPACE

Archive Information

Store old or rarely used files on a tape cartridge or a removable disk. You can then remove the files from your computer to provide more storage space.

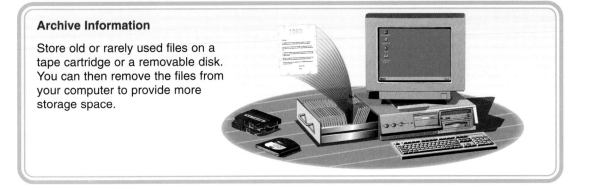

FAT32

You may be able to convert your hard drive to the FAT32 file system to better manage data on the drive and reduce wasted space. For example, converting a 1 GB drive to FAT32 may increase the amount of free space on the drive by over 200 MB.

Windows 98 includes a program you can use to convert your drive to FAT32.

Data Compression

You can compress, or squeeze together, the files stored on a hard drive. This can double the amount of information the drive can store.

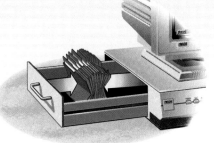

You should only compress a hard drive if it is running out of space to store new information and you have tried all other ways of increasing the available storage space.

Most operating systems include a data compression program.

A floppy drive stores data on floppy disks, or diskettes. A floppy disk is a removable device that magnetically stores data.

All computers have a floppy drive, called drive A.

Floppy Disk

Floppy drives use 3.5 inch floppy disks. Inside a 3.5 inch floppy disk is a thin, plastic, flexible disk that magnetically records data. The word floppy refers to this flexible disk.

Inside a Floppy Drive

When you insert a floppy disk into a floppy drive, the flexible disk inside the floppy disk spins. The floppy drive has read/write heads that move across the flexible disk to read and record data on the disk.

Install New Programs

Programs you buy at a computer store can come on one or several floppy disks. Before you can use a program, you must install, or copy, the contents of the floppy disks onto your computer.

Transfer Data

You can use floppy disks to transfer data from one computer to another. This lets you give data to friends and colleagues.

Back Up Important Files

You can copy important files to floppy disks. The disks will serve as backup copies if your hard drive fails or if you accidentally erase the files.

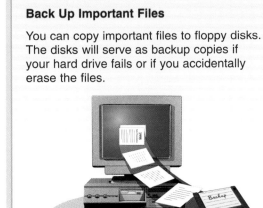

Increase Hard Drive Space

You can increase the available space on your computer by copying old or rarely used files to floppy disks. You can then remove the files from your computer to provide more storage space.

FLOPPY DRIVE

INSERT A FLOPPY DISK

Push the floppy disk gently into the drive, label side up. Most drives make a "click" sound when you have fully inserted the disk.

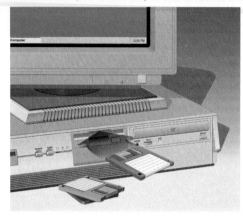

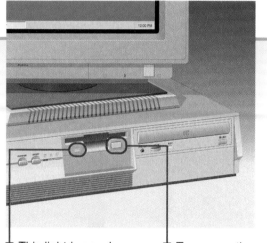

■ This light is on when the computer is using the floppy disk. Do not remove the disk when this light is on.

■ To remove the floppy disk, press this button.

PROTECT A FLOPPY DISK

You can prevent erasing and recording data on a floppy disk by sliding the tab to the write-protected position.

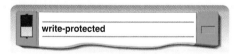

write-protected

You **cannot** erase and record data.

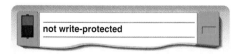

not write-protected

You **can** erase and record data.

Make sure you keep floppy disks away from magnets, which can damage the data stored on the disks. Also make sure you do not store floppy disks in extremely hot or cold locations and try not to spill liquids such as coffee or soda on the disks.

Floppy Disk Capacity

Floppy disks come in two storage capacities. High-density disks store more data than double-density disks.

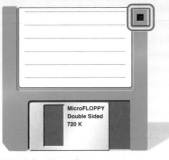
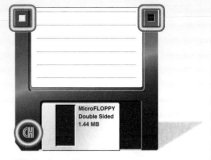

Double-density

A double-density (DD) floppy disk can store 720 K of data. This disk has only one hole at the top of the disk.

High-density

A high-density (HD) floppy disk can store 1.44 MB of data. This disk has two holes at the top of the disk and usually displays the letters HD.

Formatted Floppy Disk

A floppy disk must be formatted before you can use it to store data. Formatting a disk prepares the disk for use by dividing it into tracks and sectors. This organizes the disk so the computer can store and retrieve data.

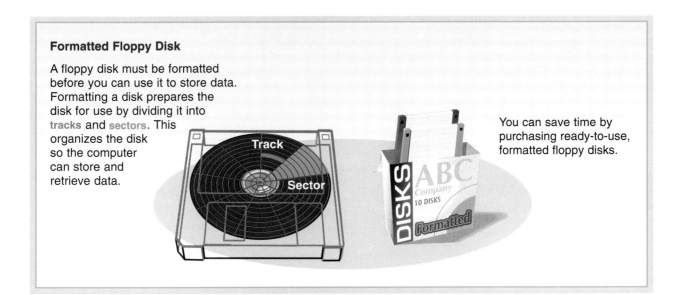

You can save time by purchasing ready-to-use, formatted floppy disks.

REMOVABLE DRIVE

A removable drive is a storage device that allows you to store large amounts of data on removable disks.

Removable disks are similar in size and shape to floppy disks.

REMOVABLE DRIVE APPLICATIONS

Archive Data

You can use a removable drive to store old or rarely used files. You can then remove the files from your computer to provide more storage space.

Protect Data

You can use a removable drive to store confidential data or backup copies of data. You can then protect the data by placing the disks in a safe place at night and on weekends.

Transfer Data

You can use a removable drive to transfer large amounts of data between computers. For example, you can take work home or transfer data to a colleague.

When using a removable drive to transfer data, you must ensure that the person receiving the data uses the same type of drive. Most removable drives cannot use disks from a different type of drive.

TYPES OF REMOVABLE DRIVES

There are several popular types of removable drives. Many new computers now come with built-in removable drives.

Jaz® Drive

Jaz® drives are currently one of the most popular types of removable drives. Jaz® drives are very fast and have the largest storage capacity of all removable drives. Some Jaz® drives can store up to 2 GB of data on a single disk.

SyJet Drive

A SyJet drive is a very fast removable drive. A SyJet drive can store up to 1.5 GB of data on a single cartridge.

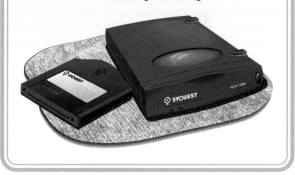

Zip® Drive

Zip® drives are currently a very popular type of removable drive. A Zip® drive is relatively inexpensive and can store up to 100 MB of data on a single disk.

SuperDisk Drive

A SuperDisk drive can store up to 120 MB of data on a single disk. Unlike many other removable drives, SuperDisk drives also accept regular 3.5 inch floppy disks.

A tape drive is a device that copies files from a computer onto tape cartridges.

Tape drives are also called tape backup units.

A tape drive can be inside the computer case or connected to the computer by a cable. An external tape drive is more expensive, but can be used with more than one computer.

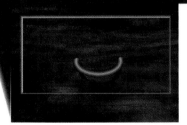

Tape Cartridges

A tape drive stores information on tape cartridges. These cartridges are similar to the cassettes you buy at music stores.

Store all cartridges in a cool, dry place, away from electrical equipment.

Back Up Data

Most people use tape drives to make backup copies of files stored on a computer. This provides extra copies in case the original files are stolen or damaged due to viruses or computer failure. Most people should back up their work every day.

Archive Data

You can copy old or rarely used files from your computer to tape cartridges. You can then remove the files from your computer to provide more storage space.

Transfer Data

You can use a tape drive to transfer large amounts of information between computers. Make sure the person receiving the information uses the same type of tape drive.

TAPE DRIVE

A backup program helps you copy the files stored on your computer to tape cartridges.

Most tape drives come with a backup program specifically designed for use with the tape drive. Most operating systems also include a backup program.

Schedule Backups

You can set a backup program to run automatically. This lets you schedule a backup at night, when you are not using your computer.

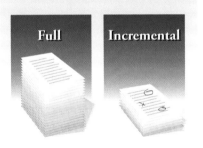

Types of Backups

A full backup will back up all your files. An incremental backup will back up only the files that have changed since the last backup. An incremental backup saves you time when backing up a lot of information.

Compress Data

A backup program can compress, or squeeze together, data you are backing up. This may allow you to double the amount of data you can store on a tape cartridge.

CHOOSE A TAPE DRIVE

When buying a tape drive, you should choose a drive that can store the entire contents of your hard drive on a single tape cartridge. This will make it easier to perform a backup of all the information on your hard drive.

Travan Drive

Travan drives are the most common type of tape drive. There are several levels of Travan drives and tape cartridges, including TR-1, TR-2, TR-3 and TR-4. The higher the level, the more data the drive or tape cartridge can store. Travan drives can accept different levels of tape cartridges. A high-quality Travan drive can store up to 10 GB of data on a single Travan cartridge.

DAT Drive

A Digital Audio Tape (DAT) drive is faster than a Travan drive, but is more expensive. A high-quality DAT drive can store up to 24 GB of data on a single DAT cartridge.

TAPE CARTRIDGES TIP

Companies often advertise the amount of compressed data a tape cartridge can store. Companies assume that compression will double the amount of information a cartridge can store. This is not always the case.

The amount of information that is actually compressed depends on the type of information you are storing. For example, a text file will compress significantly more than an image file.

CD-ROM DRIVE

A CD-ROM drive is a device that reads information stored on compact discs.

Most CD-ROM drives are located inside the computer case. External CD-ROM drives that connect to the computer by a cable are also available.

CD-ROM DISC

A CD-ROM disc is the same type of disc you buy at a music store.

A single CD-ROM disc can store more than 600 MB of data. This is equal to an entire set of encyclopedias or over 400 floppy disks. The large storage capacity of CD-ROM discs leaves more room for storing large images, animation and video.

CD-ROM stands for Compact Disc-Read-Only Memory. Read-only means you cannot change the information stored on a disc.

Install Programs

The large storage capacity of a CD-ROM disc makes installing new programs on your computer easy. A program that requires 20 floppy disks can easily fit on a single CD-ROM disc.

Play Multimedia CD-ROM Discs

A CD-ROM disc can store multimedia presentations. Multimedia refers to the combination of text, images, sound, animation and video. Multimedia provides a powerful way of communicating information.

There are thousands of multimedia CD-ROM discs available to inform and entertain you. You can buy multimedia CD-ROM discs at most computer stores.

Play Music CDs

You can play music CDs on a CD-ROM drive while you work.

CD-ROM DRIVE

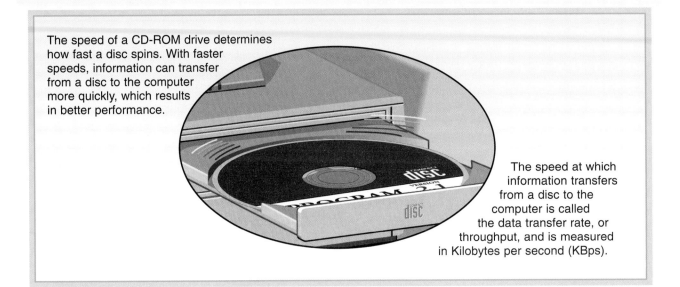

The speed of a CD-ROM drive determines how fast a disc spins. With faster speeds, information can transfer from a disc to the computer more quickly, which results in better performance.

The speed at which information transfers from a disc to the computer is called the data transfer rate, or throughput, and is measured in Kilobytes per second (KBps).

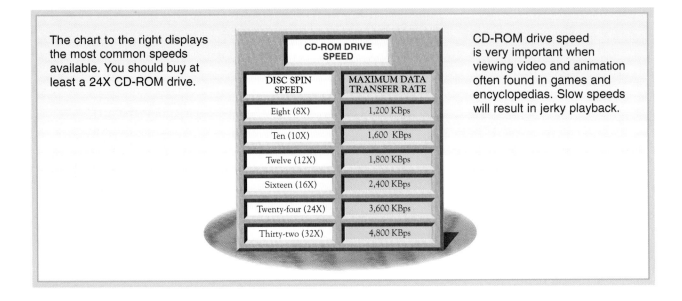

The chart to the right displays the most common speeds available. You should buy at least a 24X CD-ROM drive.

CD-ROM DRIVE SPEED	
DISC SPIN SPEED	MAXIMUM DATA TRANSFER RATE
Eight (8X)	1,200 KBps
Ten (10X)	1,600 KBps
Twelve (12X)	1,800 KBps
Sixteen (16X)	2,400 KBps
Twenty-four (24X)	3,600 KBps
Thirty-two (32X)	4,800 KBps

CD-ROM drive speed is very important when viewing video and animation often found in games and encyclopedias. Slow speeds will result in jerky playback.

WORK WITH A CD-ROM DISC

Insert a Disc

■ To insert or remove a disc, press this button.

■ A tray slides out. Place the disc, label side up, on the tray. To close the tray, press the button again.

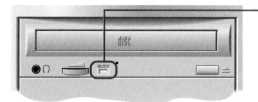

■ This light is on when the CD-ROM drive is accessing information on the disc. Do not remove the disc or move the computer when this light is on.

Headphones

You can use headphones to listen to recorded sounds on a disc. Headphones are useful in noisy environments or when you want to listen to a disc privately.

Handle a Disc

When handling a CD-ROM disc, hold the disc around the edges.

Protect a Disc

When you finish using a disc, make sure you place the disc back in its protective case. Do not stack discs on top of each other.

CD-ROM DRIVE

A CD-R (Compact Disc-Recordable) drive is a device that allows you to permanently store information on a compact disc.

A CD-R drive can also read CD-ROM discs and play music CDs.

CD-R Drive Applications

Store and Transfer Data

You can use a CD-R drive to store up to 650 MB of data on a single disc. This lets you easily transfer data, such as software applications or multimedia presentations, between computers.

CD-R discs are not erasable, so any data recorded onto a disc is permanent and cannot be changed.

Record Audio

A CD-R drive lets you create audio CDs that you can play on a CD-ROM drive or on a regular CD player. To record sound from a music CD or cassette onto a CD-R disc, you can attach your stereo system to your computer. A single CD-R disc can store up to 74 minutes of audio.

CD-R Software

A CD-R drive requires special software to record data onto a CD-R disc. Many CD-R drives come with software specifically designed for use with the drive. You can also purchase software that provides more features, such as utilities to improve the quality of the sound you are recording.

Write Speed   Read Speed

CD-R Drive Speed

A CD-R drive operates at two different speeds. The write speed refers to how fast the drive can record data onto a disc. Common CD-R drive write speeds include 2X and 4X. The read speed refers to how fast data transfers from a disc to the computer. Common CD-R drive read speeds include 6X, 8X and 12X.

CD-RW DRIVE

A CD-RW (Compact Disc-ReWritable) drive is similar to a CD-R drive, but allows you to change the data you record on a disc many times. A CD-RW disc stores the same amount of data as a CD-R disc.

Discs created on CD-RW drives may not work in some CD-R drives, CD-ROM drives or CD players.

DVD-ROM DRIVE

A DVD-ROM drive is a device that reads information stored on DVD-ROM or CD-ROM discs.

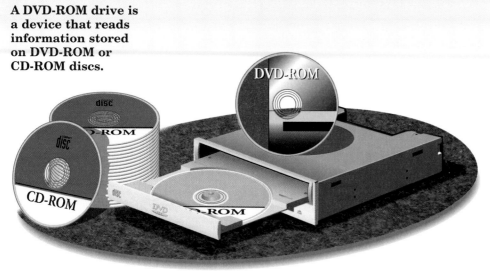

DVD-ROM stands for Digital Versatile Disc-Read-Only Memory. Read-only means you cannot change the information stored on a disc.

A DVD-ROM disc is similar in size and shape to a CD-ROM disc, but can store a lot more information.

Multimedia

You can use a DVD-ROM drive to read multimedia DVD-ROM and CD-ROM discs. A DVD-ROM drive can also play music CDs. Some DVD-ROM drives, called second generation drives, can also read CDs recorded on CD-R and CD-RW drives.

DVD-Video

DVD-ROM drives can play DVD-Video discs, which hold full-length, full-screen movies with much better quality than VHS tapes. Many DVD-Video discs allow you to change the way you view the movie, such as displaying subtitles.

You may need special hardware, such as an MPEG-2 video decoder card, for the best playback of DVD-Video.

DVD CONSIDERATIONS

DVD Disc Storage Capacity

A single DVD disc can store at least 4.7 GB of data, which equals over seven CD-ROM discs.

DVD DISC	1 side/ 1 layer	1 side/ 2 layers	2 sides/ 1 layer	2 sides/ 2 layers
Storage	4.7 GB	8.5 GB	9.4 GB	17 GB

Unlike CD-ROM discs, DVD discs can be single-sided or double-sided. Each side can store one or two layers of data.

DVD-ROM Drive Speed

The speed of a DVD-ROM drive determines how quickly data can transfer from a disc to the computer. Many DVD-ROM drives, called 1X drives, have a speed equivalent to an 8X CD-ROM drive. Newer DVD-ROM drives, called 2X drives, can reach speeds equivalent to a 24X CD-ROM drive.

RECORDABLE DVD DRIVE

Recordable DVD drives allow you to record data on DVD discs. Most recordable DVD drives are rewritable, which means you can change the data recorded on the disc. Most recordable DVD drives can also read DVD, CD-ROM, CD-R and CD-RW discs, as well as play music CDs.

CHAPTER 5

Portable Computers

Wondering what to look for in a portable computer? This chapter will provide all the information you need.

INTRODUCTION TO NOTEBOOK COMPUTERS

A notebook is a small, lightweight computer that you can easily transport.

A notebook computer is also called a laptop.

You can buy a notebook computer with the same capabilities as a desktop computer, although notebook computers are more expensive.

A notebook computer has a built-in keyboard, pointing device and screen. This eliminates the need for cables to connect these devices to the notebook.

ADVANTAGES OF NOTEBOOKS

Travel

A notebook computer lets you work when traveling or outdoors. You can also use a notebook computer to bring work home instead of staying late at the office.

Presentations

You can bring a notebook computer to meetings to present information.

A battery or an electrical outlet can supply the power for a notebook computer.

A battery lets you use a notebook when no electrical outlets are available.

TYPES OF BATTERIES

There are two main types of batteries—nickel metal hydride (NiMH) and lithium-ion. Lithium-ion is a more expensive battery, but is lighter and lasts longer than NiMH. Some notebook computers now use Smart batteries. Smart batteries help notebooks better manage power consumption.

MONITOR A BATTERY

Most notebooks display the amount of battery power remaining, either on the screen or on a panel built into the computer.

RECHARGE A BATTERY

The power supplied by most batteries lasts for only a few hours. You must recharge a battery before you can use it again. If you are unable to recharge a battery when traveling, bring an extra battery so you can work for a longer period of time.

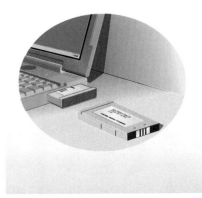

The screen on a notebook computer uses Liquid Crystal Display (LCD). This is the same type of display found in most digital wristwatches.

An LCD screen uses very little power, which extends the length of time you can use a battery before needing to recharge. An LCD screen also weighs much less than a desktop monitor, which makes a notebook easier to carry.

BACKLIGHT

Notebooks have an internal light source that illuminates the back of the screen. This makes the screen easier to view in poorly lit areas but shortens the length of time you can use a battery before needing to recharge.

POWER A FULL-SIZE MONITOR

Most notebooks can use both the notebook screen and a full-size monitor at the same time. This feature is very useful when delivering presentations.

SCREEN SIZE

The size of the screen is measured diagonally. Screen sizes range from about 12 to 15 inches.

Passive Matrix

This type of screen is less expensive than an active matrix screen, but is not as bright or rich in color. The lower cost makes a passive matrix screen ideal for routine office tasks.

A passive matrix screen is also called a Double SuperTwisted Nematic (DSTN) screen.

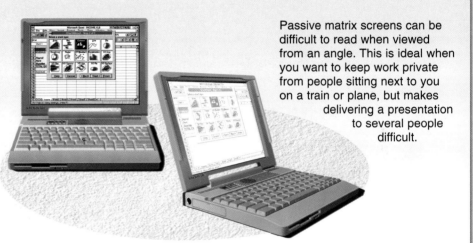

Passive matrix screens can be difficult to read when viewed from an angle. This is ideal when you want to keep work private from people sitting next to you on a train or plane, but makes delivering a presentation to several people difficult.

Active Matrix

This type of screen is more expensive, but displays brighter, richer colors than a passive matrix screen.

An active matrix screen is also called a Thin-Film Transistor (TFT) screen.

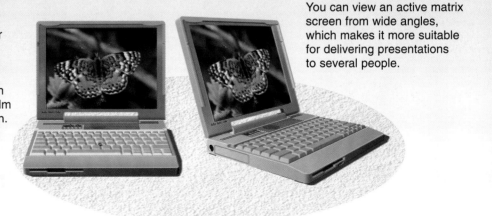

You can view an active matrix screen from wide angles, which makes it more suitable for delivering presentations to several people.

INPUT AND OUTPUT DEVICES

There are several devices that let you move the pointer around the screen of a notebook computer.

A mouse is impractical when traveling, since you need a relatively large, flat surface to move the mouse.

Pointing Stick

A pointing stick is a small, eraser-like device that you push in different directions to move the pointer on the screen.

Trackball

A trackball is an upside-down mouse that remains stationary. You roll the ball with your fingers or palm to move the pointer on the screen. Built-in trackballs on the right side of the keyboard may be awkward for left-handed users.

Touchpad

A touchpad is a surface that is sensitive to pressure and motion. When you move your fingertip across the pad, the pointer on the screen moves in the same direction.

KEYBOARD

The keys on a notebook keyboard may be small and close together to save space. Before buying a notebook, type several paragraphs of text to make sure the keyboard is suitable for you.

Some notebook computers have a keyboard that expands to a full-size keyboard.

SOUND CARD AND SPEAKERS

You can buy a notebook with a built-in sound card and speakers to play and record sound. This is very useful when you want to use the notebook to deliver presentations.

MODEM

You can buy a notebook with a built-in modem or add modem capabilities later.

A modem allows you to connect to the Internet to exchange information and messages.

When traveling, a modem also lets you connect to the network at work.

STORAGE DEVICES

HARD DRIVE

The hard drive is the primary device a notebook uses to store information. Buy the largest hard drive you can afford. New programs and data will quickly fill a hard drive.

CD-ROM OR DVD-ROM DRIVE

A notebook computer can include a CD-ROM drive or a DVD-ROM drive to read information stored on Compact Discs (CDs) or Digital Versatile Discs (DVDs).

Some notebooks let you remove the CD-ROM or DVD-ROM drive and replace it with another component. This new component could be an extra battery to increase the amount of time you can use the notebook, a second hard drive for additional storage space or a floppy drive.

FLOPPY DRIVE

Many notebooks come with a floppy drive to store and retrieve information on floppy disks.

If you will not use a floppy drive very often, you can buy a notebook without a floppy drive to reduce the notebook's weight. You can then connect the notebook to an external floppy drive when necessary.

CPU

The Central Processing Unit (CPU) is the main chip in a computer. The CPU processes instructions, performs calculations and manages the flow of information through a computer system.

The most popular CPUs for notebook computers are made by Intel. Other companies that make CPUs for notebooks include AMD and Cyrix.

This chart shows the most common CPU chips available for notebook computers. Which chip you decide to buy depends on your budget and how you plan to use the computer.

pentium II
intel.

CPU	SPEED (MHz)
Pentium with MMX	150 166 200 233
Pentium II	233 266

MEMORY

Electronic memory, or RAM, temporarily stores data inside a computer. Memory works like a blackboard that is constantly overwritten with new data. A notebook computer running Windows 98 should have at least 32 MB of memory to ensure that programs run smoothly.

PC CARD

A PC Card adds a new capability, such as sound or additional memory, to a notebook computer.

Some PC Cards provide multiple features. For example, a single PC Card can provide networking and modem capabilities.

A PC Card used to be called a PCMCIA Card. PCMCIA stands for Personal Computer Memory Card International Association.

Types of PC Cards

A PC Card is a lightweight device about the size of a credit card. There are three types of PC Cards—Type I, Type II and Type III. Type I is the thinnest card, while Type III is the thickest. Each type of card can vary in the features it offers.

Some notebooks support a new type of PC Card, called a CardBus card. These cards enhance a notebook's ability to perform demanding tasks, such as videoconferencing.

PC Slot

You insert a PC Card into a slot on a notebook computer. Most notebook computers have a PC slot that can accept both a Type I and Type II PC Card or one Type III PC Card.

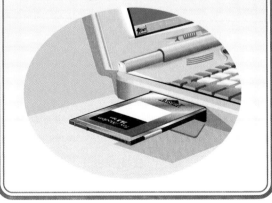

Network Interface Card

A network interface card connects a notebook to a network and controls the flow of information between the network and the notebook. When connected to a network, you can access all the equipment and information available on the network.

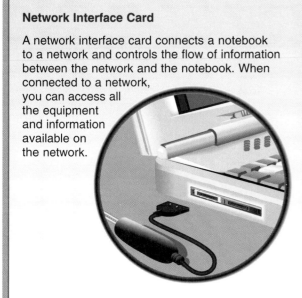

Infrared Port

Some notebook computers have an infrared port to share information without using cables. Infrared ports are commonly used for connecting a notebook computer to a printer.

Port Replicator

A port replicator lets you connect many devices, such as a printer, modem and mouse, to a notebook at once. After you connect a notebook to a port replicator, you can use all the devices attached to the port replicator without having to attach each device to the notebook individually.

Docking Station

A docking station lets you connect many devices to a notebook at once. A docking station can also provide additional features, such as networking capabilities and a full-size monitor and keyboard.

INTRODUCTION TO HANDHELD COMPUTERS

A handheld computer is a portable computer small enough to carry in your hand. A handheld computer is also called a Personal Digital Assistant (PDA) or pocket computer.

Handheld computers are capable of storing thousands of addresses, appointments and memos. You can use a handheld computer to exchange electronic mail, send and receive faxes and browse the World Wide Web. Some handheld computers also come with word processing and spreadsheet applications.

Transferring Appointments

You can connect a handheld computer to a desktop computer to exchange data between the two computers.

INPUT DEVICES

Keyboard

Handheld computers have a small keyboard that allows you to input data.

Stylus

Instead of a mouse, handheld computers use an electronic pen, called a stylus, to select objects on the screen.

Modem

You can buy a handheld computer with a built-in modem or you can add modem capabilities later. A modem allows you to connect to the Internet.

OPERATING SYSTEM

Most handheld computers use the Microsoft Windows CE operating system to control the overall activity of the computer. Windows CE is a Graphical User Interface (GUI, pronounced "gooey"). A GUI allows you to use pictures instead of text commands to perform tasks. The latest version of Windows CE comes with limited versions of popular Microsoft Office applications.

PALM COMPUTERS

Palm computers are small handheld computers that are often used as electronic organizers. You can connect a palm computer to a desktop computer to exchange data between the two computers.

Palm computers have many of the same features as handheld computers, but they do not have a keyboard. You use a stylus, or electronic pen, to input data into a palm computer.

Like handheld computers, palm computers also use an operating system to control the overall activity of the computer. Some palm computers use the Windows CE operating system, but there are other operating systems available.

Popular palm computers include 3COM's PalmPilot and Palm III.

CHAPTER 6

Software

Ready to start that report? Browse through this chapter to discover how software can help you get the job done.

INTRODUCTION TO SOFTWARE

Software helps you accomplish specific tasks.

You can use software to write letters, manage your finances, draw pictures, play games and much more.

Software is also called an application or a program.

Get Software

You can buy software at computer stores. There are also thousands of programs available on the Internet.

Install Software

Software you buy at a computer store may come on a CD-ROM disc, a DVD-ROM disc or several floppy disks. Before you can use the software, you must install, or copy, the contents of the disc or disks onto your computer. Using a CD-ROM or DVD-ROM disc is a fast method of installing software.

Software Version

Software developers and manufacturers constantly make corrections (called bug-fixes) and add new features to the software they create. When a manufacturer releases updated software, the software is given a new version number. This helps people distinguish new versions of the software from older versions.

Bundled Software

Bundled software is software that comes with a new computer system or device, such as a printer. Companies often include bundled software to let you start using the new equipment right away. For example, new computer systems usually come with word processing, spreadsheet and graphics programs.

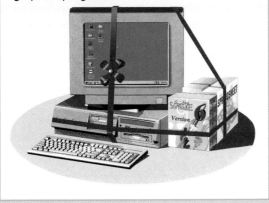

Get Help

Most software comes with a built-in help feature and printed documentation to help you learn to use the software. You can also buy computer books with detailed, step-by-step instructions at computer or book stores.

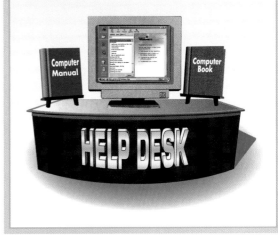

A word processor helps you create professional-looking documents quickly and efficiently.

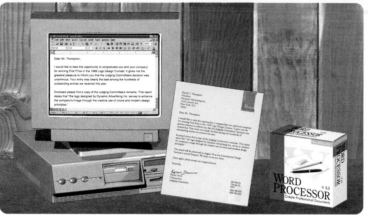

Popular word processing programs include Microsoft Word, Corel WordPerfect and Lotus Word Pro.

WORD PROCESSING HIGHLIGHTS

Documents

You can create many different types of documents, such as letters, reports, manuals, newsletters and brochures.

Tables

You can create tables to neatly organize information in a document. You can also add colors and borders to enhance the appearance of tables.

Mail Merge

Word processors offer a merge feature that lets you quickly produce personalized letters, envelopes and mailing labels for each person on a mailing list.

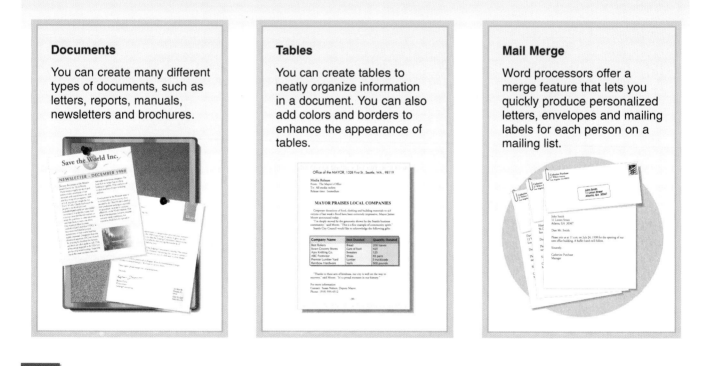

Insertion Point

The flashing line on a screen is called the insertion point. The insertion point indicates where the text you type will appear.

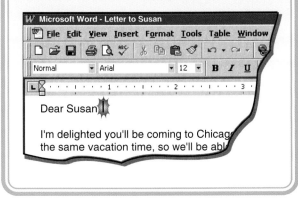

Word Wrap

A word processor automatically moves text you type to the next line. This is called word wrapping. When typing text, you need to press **Enter** only when you want to start a new paragraph.

When you use a word processor to type a letter, the text automatically wraps to the next line as you type.

Scroll

If you create a long document, the computer screen cannot display all the text at the same time. You must scroll up or down to view and edit other parts of the document.

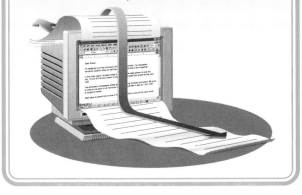

Print

You can produce a paper copy of a document. Word processors let you see on the screen exactly what a printed document will look like.

WORD PROCESSOR

Edit Text

After typing text in a document, you can easily add, delete or move text. A word processor also remembers the last changes you made to a document and lets you undo the changes.

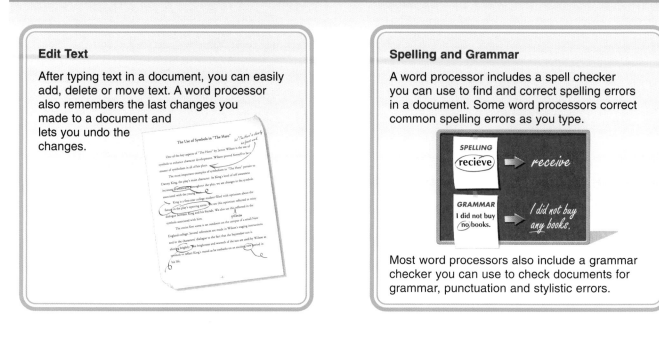

Spelling and Grammar

A word processor includes a spell checker you can use to find and correct spelling errors in a document. Some word processors correct common spelling errors as you type.

Most word processors also include a grammar checker you can use to check documents for grammar, punctuation and stylistic errors.

Thesaurus

Many word processors include a thesaurus that lets you replace a word in a document with one that is more suitable.

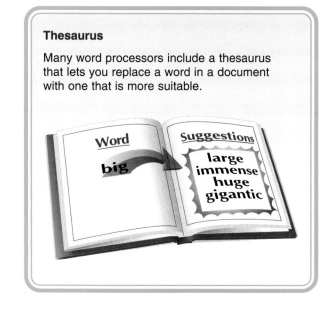

Find and Replace

You can find and replace every occurrence of a word or phrase in a document. This is useful if you have frequently misspelled a name.

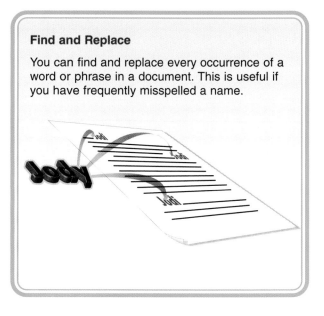

Font

Word processors include a variety of fonts you can use to create attractive documents. You can enhance the appearance of a document by changing the font, size or style of the text.

Images

Most word processors include many types of images you can use to enhance the appearance of a document. Using images can help you draw attention to important information.

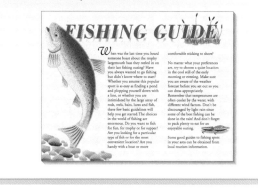

Paragraph Formatting

Word processors have many features you can use to enhance paragraphs in a document. For example, you can change the line spacing, create bulleted or numbered lists or align text in different ways.

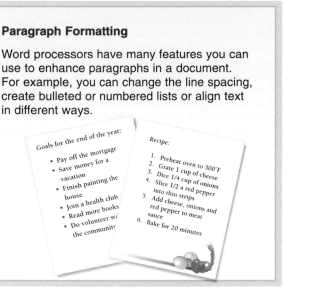

Page Formatting

You can enhance the overall appearance of pages in a document by adjusting the margin settings, adding page numbers or creating page borders.

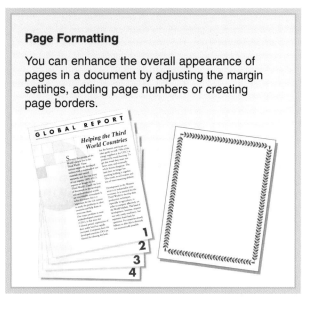

SPREADSHEET

A spreadsheet program helps you manage personal and business finances.

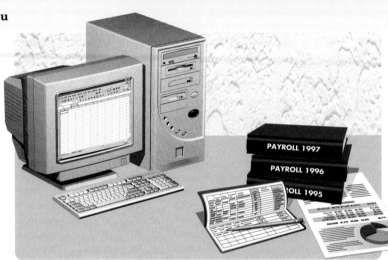

Popular spreadsheet programs include Microsoft Excel and Lotus 1-2-3.

Manage Finances

You can use a spreadsheet program to perform calculations, analyze data and present information.

Manage Data in a List

A spreadsheet program lets you store a large collection of information, such as a mailing or product list. Spreadsheet programs include tools for organizing, managing, sorting and retrieving data.

If you want greater control over a list stored on your computer, use a database program. Database programs are specifically designed to manage a list of data.

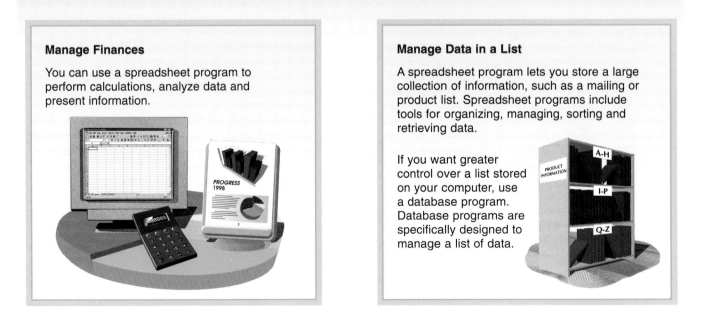

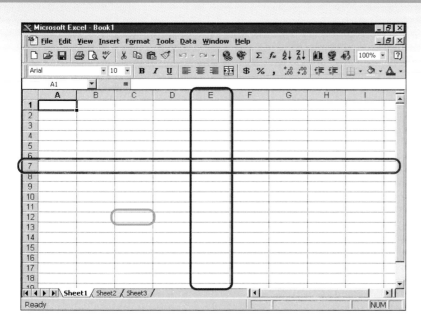

Column

A column is a vertical line of boxes. A letter identifies each column.

Row

A row is a horizontal line of boxes. A number identifies each row.

Cell

A cell is one box in a spreadsheet. You enter information into the cells in a spreadsheet.

Cell Reference

A cell reference, or cell address, defines the location of each cell in a spreadsheet. A cell reference consists of a column letter followed by a row number.

Work With Rows and Columns

You can change the width of columns and the height of rows to better fit the data in a spreadsheet. You can also insert rows and columns into a spreadsheet to add new data or delete rows and columns to remove data you no longer need.

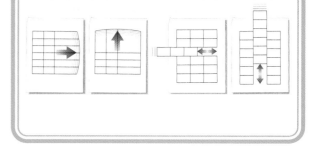

Edit Data

After entering data in a spreadsheet, you can add, delete or move the data. A spreadsheet program also remembers the last change you made and lets you undo the change.

Complete a Series

A spreadsheet program can save you time by completing a series of numbers, text or time periods for you.

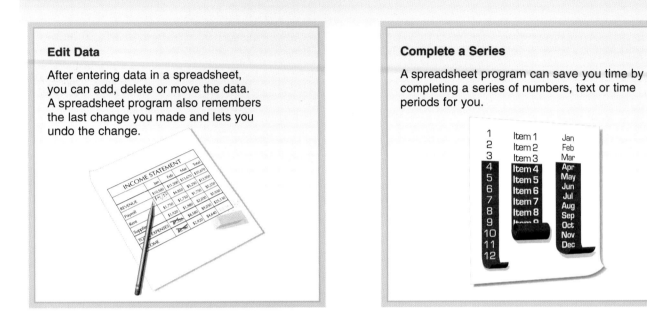

Format Data

You can change the design and size of characters to make a spreadsheet more appealing. You can also change the look and position of numbers in a spreadsheet to make them easier to read and identify.

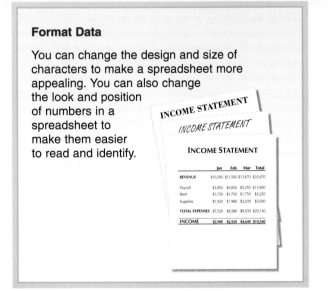

Borders, Shading and Color

You can add borders, shading and color to improve the appearance of a spreadsheet.

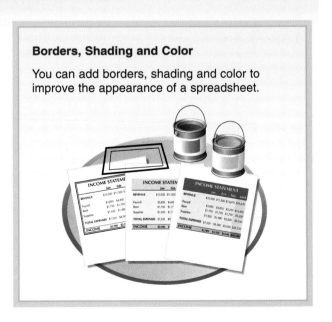

FORMULAS AND FUNCTIONS

Formula

A formula helps you calculate and analyze data in a spreadsheet. If you change a number used in a formula, you do not have to manually redo all the calculations. A spreadsheet program will automatically redo the calculations and display the new results.

Function

A function is a ready-to-use formula that helps you perform specialized calculations. For example, the SUM function adds a list of numbers. The AVERAGE function calculates the average value of a list of numbers.

CHART

Spreadsheet programs let you create charts to graphically display the data in a spreadsheet. After creating a chart, you can select a new type of chart that will better suit the data.

If you later change the data used in a chart, the spreadsheet program will automatically update the chart for you.

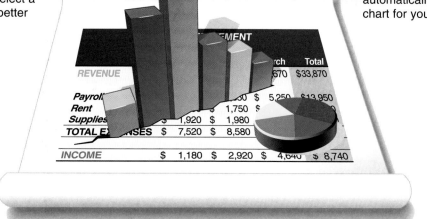

DATABASE

A database program helps you manage large collections of information.

Database programs are commonly used to manage mailing lists, phone directories, product listings and payroll information.

Popular database programs include Microsoft Access and Lotus Approach.

DATABASE APPLICATIONS

Store Information

You can use a database program to keep large collections of information organized and up-to-date.

Analyze Information

You can perform calculations on the information in a database to help you make quick, accurate and informed decisions.

Create Reports

You can use the information in a database to create professionally designed reports.

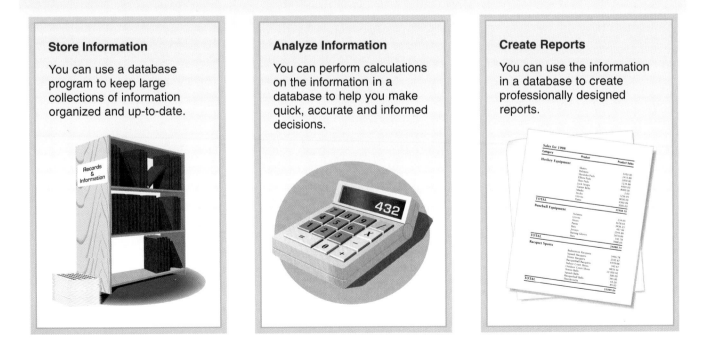

Sort

Database programs allow you to change the order of information in a database. For example, you can alphabetically sort all clients by last name. Sorting can help you keep track of the information in a database.

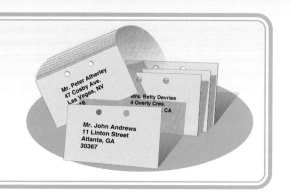

Find

You can quickly locate specific information in a database. For example, you can search for the name of a particular employee.

Query

A database program allows you to create queries to help you gather information of interest in a database. When you create a query, you ask a database program to find information that meets certain criteria, or conditions. For example, you can create a query to find employees who sold more than 1,000 units of product "A" last month.

DATABASE

Database programs store information in tables. A table is a collection of information about a specific topic, such as a mailing or product list. You can have one or more tables in a database.

Field

A field is a specific category of information in a table. For example, a field can contain the first names of all your clients.

Address ID	First Name	Last Name	Address	City	State/Province	Postal Code
1	Jim	Schmith	258 Linton Ave.	New York	NY	10010
2	Brenda	Petterson	50 Tree Lane	Boston	MA	02117
3	Todd	Talbot	68 Cracker Ave.	San Francisco	CA	94110
4	Chuck	Dean	47 Crosby Ave.	Las Vegas	NV	89116
5	Melanie	Robinson	26 Arnold Cres.	Jacksonville	FL	32256
6	Susan	Hughes	401 Idon Dr.	Nashville	TN	37243
7	Allen	Toppins	10 Heldon St.	Atlanta	GA	30375
8	Greg	Kilkenny	36 Buzzard St.	Boston	MA	02118
9	Jason	Marcuson	15 Bizzo Pl.	New York	NY	10020
10	Jim	Martin	890 Apple St.	San Diego	CA	92121

Field Name

A field name identifies the information contained in a field.

Record

A record is a collection of information about one person, place or thing in a table. For example, a record can contain the name and address of one client.

Form

Some database programs have forms you can use to easily view, enter and change information in a table. A form displays the field names in the table and all the information for one record.

TYPES OF DATABASES

Most database programs allow you to create two types of databases—flat file and relational.

EMPLOYEE PHONE NUMBERS

Name	Department	Phone Number
Allison, Steve	Accounting	555-1762
Atherly, Peter	Sales	555-2298
Boshart, Mark	Ordering	555-1270
Coleman, Dale	Sales	555-8851
Lang, Kristin	Shipping	555-9993
Lippert, Janet	Accounting	555-0042
Oram, Derek	Maintenance	555-7148
Sanvido, Dean	Service	555-0128
Smith, John	Sales	555-7018
Talbot, Mark	Ordering	555-1510

Flat File Database

A flat file database stores information in a single table.

A flat file database is easy to set up and learn. This type of database is ideal for simple lists, such as phone number and mailing lists.

Relational Database

A relational database stores information in two or more tables.

CLIENT ADDRESSES

Client #	Address	City	State
521	15 River St.	La Jolia	CA
522	82 15th Ave.	New York	NY
523	24 Ladner Cr.	Cleveland	OH
524	7 Pindar Rd.	Seattle	WA
525	60 Norfolk St.	Salem	NH
526	31 6th Ave.	New York	NY
527	116 West St.	Marietta	GA

ORDER INFORMATION

Client #	Product	Quantity
521	C28505	30
522	C48851	100
523	C33709	300
524	C40287	25
525	C58209	150
526	C48852	20
527	C29856	35

INVENTORY

Product	Price	In Stock
C28505	$80.00	12468
C48851	$20.00	1469
C33709	$30.00	50277
C40287	$45.00	6588
C58209	$19.99	206
C48852	$14.99	995
C29856	$79.00	50

Each table in a relational database contains information on a different topic, such as client addresses, order information or inventory.

The tables are related, or linked. If you change the information in one table, the same information will automatically change in all other tables.

A relational database is powerful and flexible, but can be more difficult to set up and learn than a flat file database. A relational database is ideal for invoicing, accounting and inventory.

IMAGE EDITOR

An image editor is a program that allows you to change the appearance of an image on your computer.

You can use a scanner or digital camera to transfer images to your computer. You can also obtain images from the Internet or purchase ready-made images, called clip-art, at most computer stores.

Bitmap Image

Image editors allow you to work with bitmap images. Information about bitmap images, such as color, is stored in bits. A bit is short for binary digit and is the smallest unit of data a computer can use. When you use an image editor to change the appearance of a bitmap image, you alter the bits in the image.

File Format

Bitmap images are available in many different file formats, including BMP, TIFF, JPEG and GIF. For example, many scanned images use the TIFF file format, while most images on the Internet use the JPEG or GIF file format. Most image editors are capable of opening, editing and saving images in several different file formats.

Painting Tools

Image editors provide a variety of tools you can use to paint and draw on an image.

Cut and Paste Capabilities

Image editors allow you to cut and paste parts of images to create a new image. For example, you can cut yourself out of one photo and then paste yourself in front of a famous building or beside a famous person in another photo.

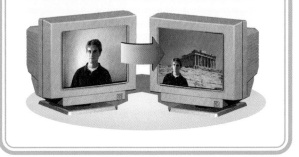

Special Effects

Many image editors let you apply special effects to an image, such as changing the shape of the image or making the image appear three-dimensional.

Photo Enhancement

Some image editors offer tools that allow you to enhance, or correct, photos, such as removing red-eye problems and increasing the brightness of photos.

A desktop publishing (DTP) program helps you create professional documents by integrating text and images on a page.

You can use a desktop publishing program to create newsletters, brochures, flyers, advertisements, magazines and books.

Popular desktop publishing programs include Adobe PageMaker, Corel Ventura and QuarkXPress.

TEXT

You can enter text directly into a desktop publishing program. You can also enter text into a word processor and then place the text in a desktop publishing document.

Word Wrap

A desktop publishing program lets you change the way text flows around an image.

Leading and Tracking

You can make text easier to read by changing the leading and tracking. Leading is the spacing between lines of text. Tracking is the space between characters.

Font

You can enhance the appearance of a document by using different character designs, sizes and styles.

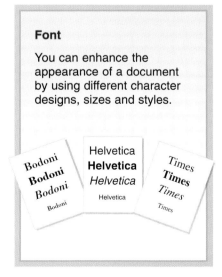

IMAGES

A desktop publishing program gives you control over the images in a document.

Get Images

Some desktop publishing programs include a collection of ready-made images, called clip art, that you can use. You can also copy images, such as photographs and drawings, into a desktop publishing document using a scanner.

Work With Images

You can move, size and rotate images in a desktop publishing document.

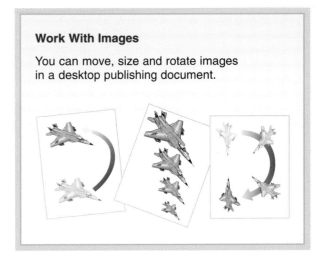

PAGE LAYOUT

A desktop publishing program has several features that can help you create pages in a document.

Master Page

A master page contains formatting that is repeated throughout a desktop publishing document, such as page numbers and headings.

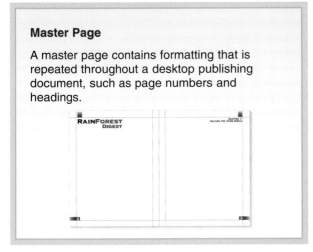

Paragraph Style

A paragraph style is a group of settings you save and then apply to sections of text in a document. Paragraph styles save you time and help give the document a consistent design.

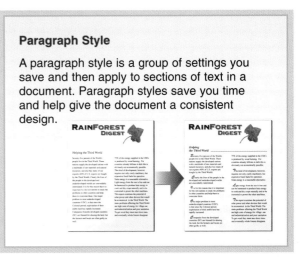

APPLICATION SUITE

An application suite is a collection of programs sold together in one package.

Cost

Buying programs as part of an application suite costs less than buying each program individually.

Easy to Use

Programs in an application suite share a common design and work in a similar way. Once you learn one program, you can easily learn the others.

DISADVANTAGE

Since all the programs in an application suite come from the same manufacturer, you may not get the best combination of features for your needs. Make sure you evaluate all the programs in an application suite before making your purchase.

APPLICATION SUITE PROGRAMS

Most application suites include four types of programs. Some application suites also offer additional programs, such as a scheduling program that lets you keep track of appointments.

Word Processing Program

A word processing program lets you create documents, such as letters and reports.

Presentation Program

A presentation program lets you design presentations.

Spreadsheet Program

A spreadsheet program lets you manage and analyze financial information.

Database Program

A database program lets you manage large collections of information. A database program may only be included in higher-priced versions of an application suite.

POPULAR APPLICATION SUITES

Microsoft Office is the most popular application suite.

Other application suites include Corel WordPerfect Suite and Lotus SmartSuite.

UTILITY SOFTWARE

A utility is a program that performs a specific task on your computer.

You can buy many utility programs at computer stores. Some utility programs are also available free of charge on the Internet.

The utilities you can use depend on the operating system running on your computer.

Norton Utilities

Symantec's Norton Utilities provides tools to help you maintain and optimize your computer. Norton Utilities also includes tools to help you recover lost files and protect against computer failure.

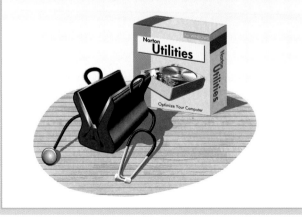

VirusScan Security Suite

McAfee's VirusScan Security Suite is a collection of anti-virus programs you can use to reduce the risk of a virus infecting your computer. A virus is a program that can cause problems ranging from displaying annoying messages on your screen to erasing the information on your hard drive.

Acrobat Reader

Adobe Acrobat Reader is a program that allows you to view Portable Document Format (.pdf) files. These files are often used on the World Wide Web to display books and magazines exactly as they appear in printed form.

ViaVoice Gold

IBM's ViaVoice Gold is a speech recognition program that allows you to control your computer with your voice. You can speak to your computer to open files or dictate documents into a word processor.

WinFax Pro

With Symantec's WinFax Pro, you can use your computer's fax modem to send and receive faxes. WinFax Pro can also convert the faxes you receive into documents that you can edit using a word processor.

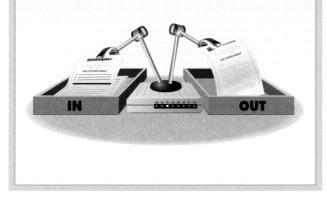

WinZip

Nico Mak's WinZip helps you decompress files. Many of the files on the Internet are compressed, or squeezed together, and must be decompressed before you can use them on your computer.

WinZip also compresses information so files can transfer faster between computers.

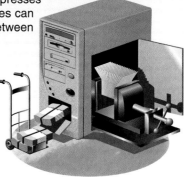

GAME SOFTWARE

Game software lets you play games on your computer. Games are a fun way to improve your reflexes and hand-eye coordination.

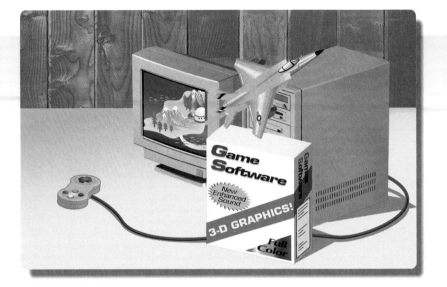

GAME HARDWARE

You may need special hardware to use game software on your computer.

Game Controller

A game controller is a device, such as a joystick or gamepad, which allows you to interact with a game. Popular game controllers include Microsoft SideWinder and Gravis GamePad.

Some games require a specific type of game controller. Before buying game software, check to see what type of controller the game requires.

3D Graphics Card

Many games are designed with 3D graphics and run best on a computer with a 3D graphics card. A 3D graphics card is a circuit board that translates complex instructions from the computer into a form the monitor can understand. Popular 3D graphics cards include Matrox Millenium and Diamond Monster 3D.

Some games require a specific type of 3D graphics card. Before buying game software, check to see what type of card the game requires.

GAME CONSIDERATIONS

Types of Games

There are many different types of games available, including action, sports, strategy, simulation, puzzle and educational games. Games are available for all ages and skill levels.

Internet and Network Games

Many games are designed to allow several people to compete against each other on the Internet or on a network.

There are many online gaming services available that allow you to easily connect to other people on the Internet to play a game. When you play a game with other people on the Internet, each person usually has to have a copy of the game.

Purchase Game Software

You can buy game software at computer stores. There are also many games available on the Internet. Game software can be very expensive, but manufacturers often offer a trial version of their game software free of charge on the World Wide Web. This lets you try a game before you buy it.

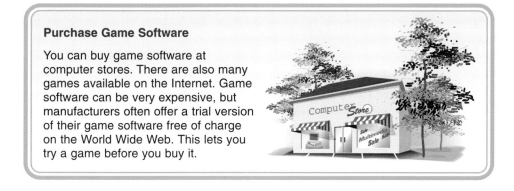

CHAPTER 7

Operating Systems

What is an operating system and which one is best for you? This chapter provides the information you are looking for.

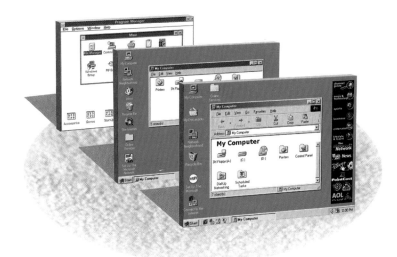

INTRODUCTION TO OPERATING SYSTEMS

An operating system is the software that controls the overall activity of a computer.

An operating system ensures that all parts of a computer system work together smoothly and efficiently.

OPERATING SYSTEM FUNCTIONS

Control Hardware

An operating system controls the different parts of a computer system and enables all the parts to work together.

Run Application Software

An operating system runs application software, such as Microsoft Word and Lotus 1-2-3.

Manage Information

An operating system provides ways to manage and organize information stored on a computer. You can use an operating system to sort, copy, move, delete or view files.

MS-DOS

MS-DOS stands for Microsoft Disk Operating System. MS-DOS displays lines of text on the screen. You perform tasks by typing short commands.

Windows

Windows displays a graphical screen. You use a mouse to perform tasks.

Windows is a Graphical User Interface (GUI, pronounced "gooey"). A GUI allows you to use pictures instead of text commands to perform tasks. This makes Windows easier to use than MS-DOS.

UNIX

UNIX is a powerful operating system used by many computers on the Internet. There are many different versions of the UNIX operating system available.

PLATFORM

A platform refers to the type of operating system used by a computer, such as MS-DOS or Windows. Programs used on one platform will not usually work on another platform.

For example, you cannot use Word for Windows on a computer running only MS-DOS.

MS-DOS is an operating system that performs tasks using text commands you enter.

MS-DOS stands for Microsoft Disk Operating System.

Command Prompt

The command prompt (C:\>) tells you that MS-DOS is ready to accept a command.

Command

You enter a command to perform a task or start a program.

A single command can usually tell the computer what you want to accomplish. For example, the DATE command tells the computer to display the current date.

Cursor

The cursor is the flashing line on the screen. The cursor indicates where the text you type will appear.

FILE ORGANIZATION

Like folders in a filing cabinet, MS-DOS uses directories to organize the data stored on a computer.

The root directory (C:\) is the main directory. All other directories are located within this directory.

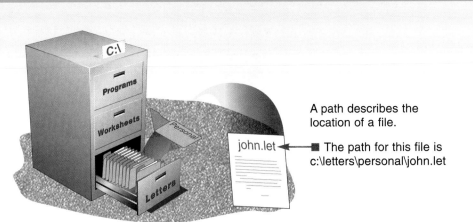

A path describes the location of a file.

■ The path for this file is c:\letters\personal\john.let

FILE NAME

When you store a file on a computer, you must give the file a name. An MS-DOS file name cannot contain any spaces. A file name consists of a name and an extension, separated by a period.

The **name** describes the contents of a file and can have up to eight characters.

The **extension** identifies the type of file and consists of three characters.

UTILITIES

Some versions of MS-DOS include special programs, called utilities, to protect files and optimize a computer. For example, one utility finds and repairs disk errors.

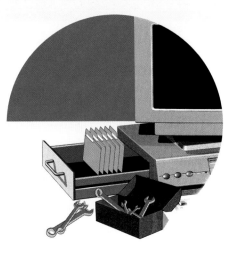

Windows 3.1 works with MS-DOS to control the overall activity of a computer. Windows 3.1 is not a true operating system since it needs MS-DOS to operate.

Windows 3.1 displays pictures on the screen to help you perform tasks.

Program Manager

The Program Manager is the control center where you start programs. The Program Manager appears on the screen each time you start Windows 3.1.

Program Icon

A program icon lets you start a program, such as a word processor. An icon is a small picture that represents an object, such as a program.

Window

A window is a rectangle that displays information on the screen. Each window has a title bar that displays the name of the window (example: Accessories).

Group Icon

A group icon contains program icons. For example, the Games group icon contains several games.

Desktop

The desktop is the background area of the screen.

Control Panel

The Control Panel lets you change the way Windows 3.1 looks and acts. For example, you can change the colors displayed on the screen.

Accessories

Windows 3.1 provides several accessories, or mini-programs, that let you accomplish simple tasks, such as writing letters and drawing pictures.

File Manager

The File Manager lets you view and organize all the files stored on a computer. Windows 3.1 uses directories to organize information, just as you would use folders to organize papers in a filing cabinet.

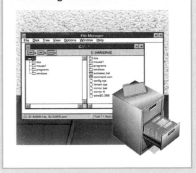

WINDOWS FOR WORKGROUPS 3.11

Windows for Workgroups (WfWG) 3.11 is a more powerful version of Windows 3.1. Like Windows 3.1, this program is not a true operating system since it needs MS-DOS to operate.

Windows for Workgroups 3.11 lets you share files and printers with other computers connected to a network and includes programs for electronic mail and scheduling.

Windows 95 is the successor to Windows 3.1. This operating system is more graphical and easier to use than Windows 3.1.

Windows 95 is a true operating system because it does not need MS-DOS to operate.

Window

A window is a rectangle that displays information on the screen. Each window has a title bar that displays the name of the window (example: My Computer).

My Computer

My Computer lets you browse through all the folders and documents stored on a computer.

Recycle Bin

The Recycle Bin stores all the documents you delete and allows you to recover them later.

Network Neighborhood

Network Neighborhood lets you view all the folders and files available on your network.

Start Button

The Start button lets you quickly access programs and documents.

Taskbar

The taskbar contains the Start button and displays the name of each open window on the screen.

Shortcut

A shortcut provides a quick way to open a document or program you use regularly.

WINDOWS 95 FEATURES

Customize Windows 95

You can easily change the way Windows 95 looks and acts. You can change the colors displayed on the screen or adjust the date and time set in the computer.

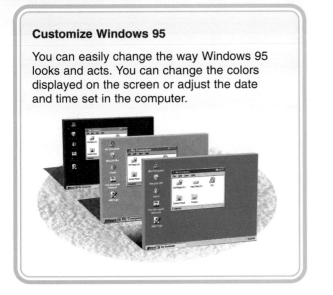

Document Names

You can use up to 255 characters, including spaces, to name a document in Windows 95. This lets you give your documents descriptive names so they are easy to identify.

Plug and Play

Windows 95 supports Plug and Play technology. This technology lets you add new features to a computer without complex and time-consuming installation procedures.

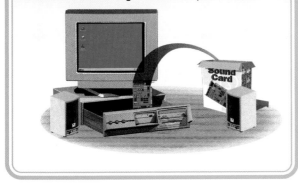

Windows Explorer

Like a map, Windows Explorer shows you the location of each folder and document on a computer. You can use Windows Explorer to move, open, print or delete documents.

WINDOWS 95

WordPad and Paint

Windows 95 comes with a word processing program, called WordPad, that lets you create simple documents such as letters and memos. Windows 95 also includes a drawing program, called Paint, that lets you create pictures.

Computer Performance

Windows 95 comes with several features that will improve the performance of a computer. For example, the ScanDisk feature finds and repairs hard disk errors.

Backup

The Backup feature lets you copy important information stored on a computer to floppy disks or tape cartridges. This helps protect the information in case the original files are stolen or damaged due to viruses or computer failure.

Briefcase

The Briefcase feature lets you easily transfer files between your office and a portable computer. This feature is useful if you work at home or while traveling. When you return to the office, Briefcase will update any documents you changed.

Microsoft Exchange

Windows 95 comes with Microsoft Exchange. This feature lets you exchange electronic mail with other people on a network or the Internet. You can also use this feature to send faxes to other computers or fax machines.

Networking

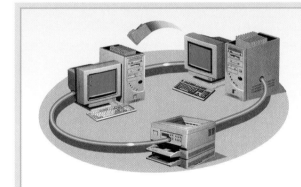

Windows 95 comes with features that let you share information and printers on a network. The Network Neighborhood feature lets you browse through and access information on all computers on a network. When at home or traveling, you can use the Dial-Up Networking feature to access information on the office network.

OSR2

OSR2 is the most recent version of Windows 95 and contains many enhancements to the original version. Some of the new features available in OSR2 include Internet applications and a program that allows you to work with scanned documents. Although you cannot purchase the entire OSR2 operating system, you can get individual OSR2 features on the Internet.

Windows 98 is the successor to Windows 95. This operating system is similar to Windows 95, but includes many new and improved features.

If you have used Windows 95, you will already be familiar with the way Windows 98 looks and works.

My Documents

My Documents provides a convenient place to store your documents.

Internet Explorer

Internet Explorer lets you browse through information on the World Wide Web.

Quick Launch Toolbar

The Quick Launch Toolbar lets you quickly access commonly used features, including Internet Explorer, Outlook Express, the desktop and special Web sites, called channels.

Window

A window is a rectangle that displays information on the screen. A window often displays a description of the selected item in the window. Most windows also display a toolbar containing buttons you can use to work with items in the window.

Channel Bar

The Channel Bar provides access to special Web sites, called channels, that Windows can automatically deliver to your computer.

Computer Maintenance

Windows 98 is more reliable than Windows 95 and includes many tools you can use to find and fix problems with your computer.

For example, you can use the Maintenance Wizard to perform maintenance tasks on a regular basis, such as checking your hard disk for errors, removing unnecessary files and defragmenting your hard disk to improve its performance.

Computer Optimization

Windows 98 includes many improved features to help you optimize your computer's performance.

For example, the advanced compression utilities in Windows 98 will help you increase the amount of information your hard drive can store.

FAT32

FAT32 is a file system that better manages data on large hard drives to reduce wasted space. Windows 98 can convert your hard drive to FAT32 without disrupting your current programs and documents.

Customize Windows 98

Windows 98 offers a large selection of visual effects and desktop themes you can use to customize the way Windows looks. You can customize the appearance of folders by adding a picture to the folder's background. Windows 98 also allows you to view your desktop as a Web page.

Multiple Monitor Capability

Windows 98 has the ability to display the Windows desktop on multiple monitors. This makes working with several open documents or programs easier.

WebTV

Windows 98 makes your computer more entertaining by including a program called WebTV. You can use WebTV to watch your favorite television shows on your computer.

Windows Update

Windows 98 provides the Windows Update feature, which lets you access the Windows Update page on the World Wide Web for the latest software updates, new features and technical support information.

Internet Explorer

Windows 98 includes Internet Explorer 4.0, which is a program that enables you to browse through the information on the World Wide Web. For more information about Internet Explorer, see page 206.

Outlook Express

Windows 98 includes Outlook Express. This program allows you to exchange electronic mail with people around the world. You can exchange messages with friends, colleagues, family members and clients.

FrontPage Express

FrontPage Express is a program included with Windows 98 that you can use to create and edit your own Web pages. You can place pages you create on the Web so people around the world can view your pages.

Channels

Windows 98 enables you to access channels on the Internet. A channel is a specially designed Web site that can automatically deliver information from the Internet to your computer.

WINDOWS NT

Windows NT is the most powerful version of the Windows operating system and provides excellent security features.

Windows NT is available in two main versions.

WINDOWS NT SERVER

Windows NT Server is found on client/server networks. This version of the operating system is designed to support the heavy processing demands of a network server.

The client computers on a network running Windows NT Server can use a variety of operating systems, such as Windows 95, Windows 98 and Mac OS 8.

WINDOWS NT WORKSTATION

Windows NT Workstation is another version of the Windows NT operating system and is used on both client/server and peer-to-peer networks.

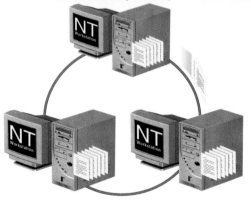

Many powerful applications are designed specifically to run on Windows NT Workstation. Many applications designed for the Windows 95 and 98 operating systems will also perform better on Windows NT Workstation.

32-bit Operating System

Both main versions of Windows NT are 32-bit operating systems. 32-bit refers to the amount of data processed at one time by the operating system. 32-bit operating systems effectively use the powerful processing capabilities of CPUs such as the Intel Pentium and Digital Alpha.

Ease of Use

The Windows NT operating system is very easy to use. Windows NT has the same look and feel as the Windows 95 and 98 operating systems.

Like other versions of Windows, Windows NT is a Graphical User Interface (GUI, pronounced "gooey"). GUIs can make many tasks easier.

Support

There are many books and software applications, as well as technical support, available for people who use the Windows NT operating system.

There are also courses designed to certify people who use and maintain the Windows NT operating system.

UNIX

UNIX is an older, powerful operating system that can be used to run a single computer or an entire network.

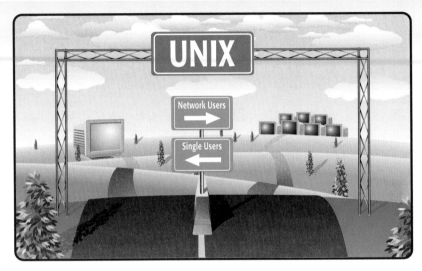

UNIX is the oldest computer operating system still in widespread use today.

VERSIONS

Many companies have owned UNIX since its development in the late 1960s. Today, there are several versions of the UNIX operating system available.

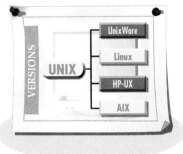

Popular UNIX operating systems for personal computers include UnixWare by SCO and Linux, which is available for free on the World Wide Web. Other versions of UNIX that are more popular as network operating systems include HP-UX by Hewlett-Packard and AIX by IBM.

INTERNET

Many of the first computers used to establish the Internet ran the UNIX operating system. Even today, UNIX is the most widely used operating system for servers on the Internet.

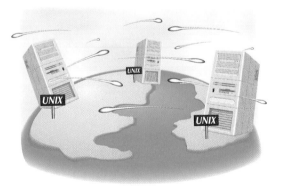

UNIX FEATURES

Power

The UNIX operating system is very powerful. UNIX is harder to install and set up than most other operating systems, but provides greater control over a computer's resources and power.

A computer's performance may be significantly improved when running UNIX.

Multitasking

UNIX was originally developed as the operating system for a single large computer, called a mainframe computer. Since multiple users can access a mainframe computer at the same time, UNIX was developed to run many programs and perform numerous tasks at once, called multitasking.

UNIX's multitasking capabilities make it an efficient operating system for networks.

Security

UNIX has many built-in security features to protect information from being accidentally deleted or accessed by unauthorized users.

UNIX's strong security features are one of the reasons UNIX is such a popular operating system on the Internet.

CHAPTER 8

Macintosh Computers

*Wondering what a Macintosh is?
This chapter will introduce you
to Macintosh computers.*

WHAT IS A MACINTOSH?

Macintosh computers, or Macs, were introduced by Apple Computer in 1984. Macintosh computers were the first home computers with a mouse, on-screen windows, menus and icons.

MACINTOSH ADVANTAGES

Easy to Use

The graphical interface of a Macintosh makes this type of computer very easy to use.

Desktop Publishing

The fast display of images on screen and true What You See Is What You Get (WYSIWYG) have helped to establish Macintosh computers as the standard in the desktop publishing industry. Desktop publishing lets you create professional documents by integrating text and graphics on a page.

The most popular types of Macintosh computers are made by Apple Computer.

Power Macintosh

The Apple Power Macintosh is available as a desktop, tower or all-in-one computer. The newest Power Macintosh is called a G3.

A desktop computer usually sits on a desk, under a monitor. A tower computer usually sits on the floor. An all-in-one computer can contain many devices, including a monitor, CD-ROM drive and speakers, in a single unit.

iMac

The iMac is Apple's newest all-in-one computer. This relatively inexpensive computer comes with all the components needed to access the Internet.

PowerBook

The Apple PowerBook is a small, lightweight computer that you can easily transport. Like other notebook computers, PowerBooks have a built-in keyboard and screen. The newest PowerBook is called a G3.

You can buy a PowerBook with the same capabilities as a full-size computer.

OPERATING SYSTEM

An operating system is the software that controls the overall activity of a computer.

Like the Windows operating systems, Macintosh operating systems use a Graphical User Interface (GUI, pronounced "gooey"). A GUI allows you to use pictures instead of text commands to perform tasks.

System 7

Older Macintosh computers use the System 7 operating system. System 7.6 was the final release of System 7.

Mac OS 8

Newer Macintosh computers use the more powerful Mac OS 8 operating system. OS 8 has many new features, including improved Internet capabilities and the ability to work with Windows and MS-DOS files. Mac OS 8.5 will be the next release of OS 8.

A port is a connector at the back of a computer where you plug in an external device.

Serial Port

A serial port connects a printer or modem.

Monitor Port

A monitor port connects a monitor.

ADB Port

An Apple Desktop Bus (ADB) port connects a keyboard or mouse.

Audio/Video Port

High-end Macintosh computers have an Audio/Video port that connects a tape deck or VCR. Low-end Macintosh computers have only a microphone port and a speaker port.

SCSI Port

A Small Computer System Interface (SCSI) port allows you to attach several separate devices to your computer. SCSI connections are very fast, which makes them ideal for connecting high-speed devices such as external hard drives and removable drives.

INPUT AND OUTPUT DEVICES

MOUSE

A mouse is a handheld pointing device that lets you select and move items on your screen. Unlike a PC mouse, which has two buttons, a Macintosh mouse has only one button.

KEYBOARD

The keys on a keyboard let you enter information and instructions into a computer. The Macintosh keyboard has a **Command**, or **Apple**, key (⌘ ⌘) that you can use to quickly perform specific tasks. For example, in a word processing document, you can quickly make text bold by pressing the ⌘ ⌘ and B keys.

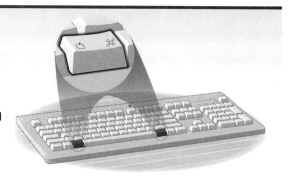

PRINTER

A printer produces a paper copy of the information displayed on the screen. When buying a printer for a Macintosh computer, make sure the printer is Macintosh-compatible. A printer designed for a PC may not work with a Mac.

MONITOR

A monitor displays text and images generated by a computer. Some monitors are designed to work only with Macintosh computers. For more flexibility, you can buy a monitor that will work with both Macs and PCs.

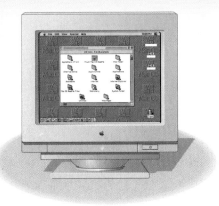

VIDEO CARD

A video card translates instructions from the computer into a form the monitor can understand. Most Macintosh computers come with a built-in video card.

SOUND CHIP

A sound chip allows a computer to play and record high-quality sound. All Macintosh computers come with a built-in sound chip.

MODEM

A modem lets computers exchange information through telephone lines. Most Macintosh modems are external modems. An external modem sits on a desk and plugs into the back of a computer.

PROCESSING

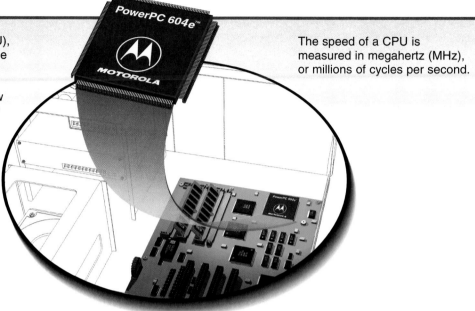

The Central Processing Unit (CPU), also called a microprocessor, is the main chip in a computer. A CPU processes instructions, performs calculations and manages the flow of information through a computer system.

All new Macintosh computers use Motorola's PowerPC™ microprocessors, also called Reduced Instruction Set Computer (RISC) chips.

The speed of a CPU is measured in megahertz (MHz), or millions of cycles per second.

TYPES OF CPUs

603e

The PowerPC™ 603e microprocessor is most often found in older portable Macintosh computers and can have speeds of up to 300 MHz.

604e

The PowerPC™ 604e microprocessor is a more powerful CPU found in older Macintosh computers and can have speeds of up to 350 MHz.

G3 (750)

The PowerPC™ 750 microprocessor is Motorola's newest CPU and can be found in Apple's new G3 computers. This new CPU can have speeds of up to 300 MHz, but includes more built-in cache, or memory, than earlier generations. This built-in cache further increases the overall speed of the CPU.

BUS

The bus is the electronic pathway in a computer that carries information between devices.

The efficiency of a bus depends on the bus width and the bus speed. Bus speed is measured in megahertz (MHz).

PCI Bus

The Peripheral Component Interconnect (PCI) bus is found in all new Macintosh computers. The PCI bus can have a width of 32 or 64 bits and speeds of up to 66 MHz.

MEMORY

Memory, also called Random Access Memory (RAM), temporarily stores data inside a computer.

The amount of memory determines the number of programs a computer can run at once and how fast programs will operate.

Capacity

Memory is measured in bytes. You should buy a Macintosh with at least 32 MB of memory, but 64 MB of memory is recommended. You can often improve the performance of a computer by adding more memory.

CHAPTER 9

Networks

How can your company share information more efficiently? Networks are explained in this chapter.

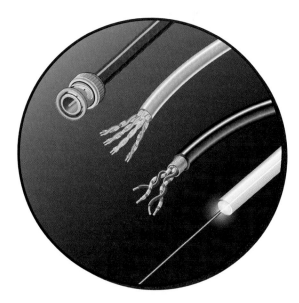

INTRODUCTION TO NETWORKS

A network is a group of connected computers that allow people to share information and equipment.

Local Area Network

A Local Area Network (LAN) is a network that connects computers within a small geographic area, such as a building.

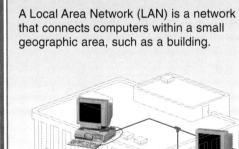

Wide Area Network

A Wide Area Network (WAN) is a network that connects computers across a large geographic area, such as a city or country. A WAN can transmit information by telephone line, microwave or satellite.

NETWORK ADVANTAGES

Work Away From Office

When traveling or at home, you can connect to the network at work to exchange messages and files.

Eliminate Sneakernet

Sneakernet refers to physically carrying information from one computer to another to exchange information. A computer network eliminates the need for sneakernet.

Share Information

Networks let you easily share data and programs. You can exchange documents, electronic mail, video, sound and images.

Share Equipment

Computers connected to a network can share equipment, such as a printer or modem.

NETWORK ADMINISTRATOR

A network administrator manages the network and makes sure the network runs smoothly. A network administrator may also be called a network manager, information systems manager or system administrator.

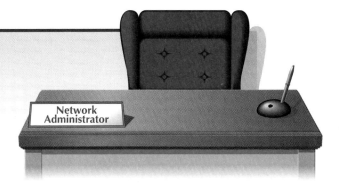

Network Administrator

NETWORK APPLICATIONS

Electronic Mail

You can exchange electronic mail (e-mail) with other people on a network. Electronic mail saves paper and provides a fast, convenient way to exchange ideas and request information.

Groupware

Groupware is software that helps people on a network coordinate and manage projects. Groupware packages usually let you exchange electronic mail, schedule meetings, participate in online discussions and share corporate information. Popular groupware packages include Lotus Domino and Novell GroupWise.

Videoconferencing

Videoconferencing allows you to have face-to-face conversations with other people on a network, whether they are around the corner or on the other side of the country.

A computer must have a sound card, speakers and a microphone to transmit and receive sound. The computer must also have a video camera to transmit video images.

Network Traffic

Network traffic is the information that travels through a network. When there is a lot of network traffic, information travels more slowly through the network.

Hub

A hub is a device that provides a central location where all the cables on a network come together.

Network Interface Card

A network interface card is a device that physically connects each computer to a network. This card controls the flow of information between the network and the computer.

Cables

Cables are the wires that connect computers and equipment on a network. There are four main types of cables—coaxial, Unshielded Twisted Pair (UTP), Shielded Twisted Pair (STP) and fiber-optic.

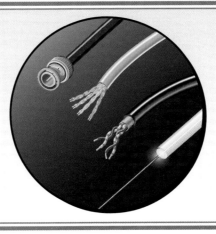

Fiber-optic cable is the most expensive type of cable, but it can carry information faster and over longer distances than other types of cables.

HOW INFORMATION IS STORED

All the people on a peer-to-peer network store their files on their own computers. Anyone on the network can access files stored on any other computer.

A peer-to-peer network provides a simple and inexpensive way to connect fewer than ten computers.

Manage Files

Files are stored in many different locations. This makes the files difficult to manage, back up and protect. However, if one computer malfunctions, the rest of the network will not be affected.

Popular Operating Systems

Popular operating systems that provide peer-to-peer networking capabilities include LANtastic, Windows for Workgroups, Windows 95 and Windows 98.

CLIENT/SERVER NETWORK

All the people on a client/server network store their files on a central computer. Everyone connected to the network can access the files stored on the central computer.

A client/server network provides a highly efficient way to connect ten or more computers or computers exchanging large amounts of information.

Server

The server is the central computer that stores the files of every person on the network.

Manage Files

All the files are stored on the server. This makes the files easy to manage, back up and protect. However, if the server malfunctions, the entire network will be affected.

Popular Operating Systems

Popular operating systems that provide client/server networking capabilities include NetWare and Windows NT.

Client

A client is a computer that can access information stored on the server.

HOW INFORMATION IS EXCHANGED

Ethernet is the most popular and least expensive way information can travel through a network. Ethernet is the easiest type of network to set up.

How Ethernet Works

Ethernet works the same way people talk during a polite conversation. Each computer waits for a pause before sending information through a network.

When two computers try to send information at the same time, a collision occurs. After a moment, the computers resend the information.

Speed

Ethernet can transfer information through a network at a speed of 10 megabits per second (Mbps). Fast Ethernet can transfer information through a network at a speed of 100 Mbps. Gigabit Ethernet is a new type of Ethernet that can transfer information through a network at a speed of 1000 Mbps.

TOKEN-RING

Token-ring is a type of network often found in large organizations, such as banks and insurance companies.

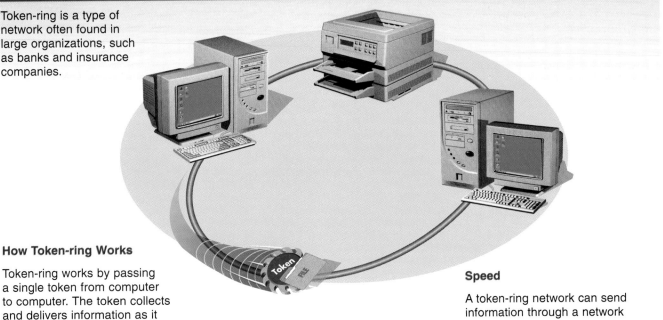

How Token-ring Works

Token-ring works by passing a single token from computer to computer. The token collects and delivers information as it travels around the network.

Speed

A token-ring network can send information through a network at speeds of 4 or 16 Mbps.

ATM

Asynchronous Transfer Mode (ATM) is a faster, more powerful way to exchange information on busy networks.

Companies often use ATM to transfer information between two separate networks.

How ATM Works

ATM works by sending information in equal-sized pieces, called cells.

Speed

ATM can send information at speeds of 25, 155 or 622 Mbps.

NETWORK SECURITY

FIREWALL

A firewall is special software or hardware designed to protect a private computer network from unauthorized access. Firewalls are used by corporations, banks and research facilities to keep information private and secure.

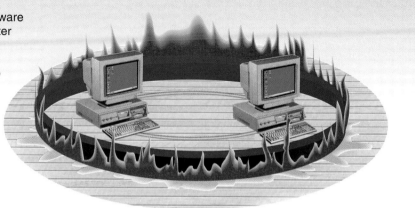

USER NAME AND PASSWORD

You usually have to enter a user name and password when you want to access information on a network. This ensures that only authorized people can use the information stored on the network.

Choose a Password

When choosing a password, do not use words that people can easily associate with you, such as your name or favorite sport. The most effective password connects two words or number sequences with a special character (example: easy@123). To increase security, memorize your password and do not write it down.

An intranet is a small version of the Internet inside an office.

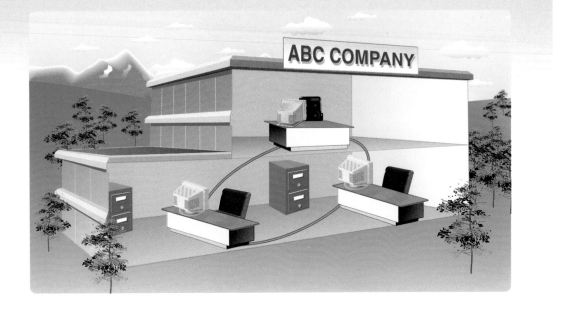

Information

An intranet is a very efficient and inexpensive way to make internal company documents available to employees. Companies use intranets to distribute information such as phone directories, product listings and job openings.

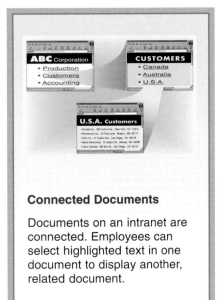

Connected Documents

Documents on an intranet are connected. Employees can select highlighted text in one document to display another, related document.

Software

The software used to exchange information on an intranet, such as a Web browser or e-mail program, is the same as the software used to exchange information on the Internet.

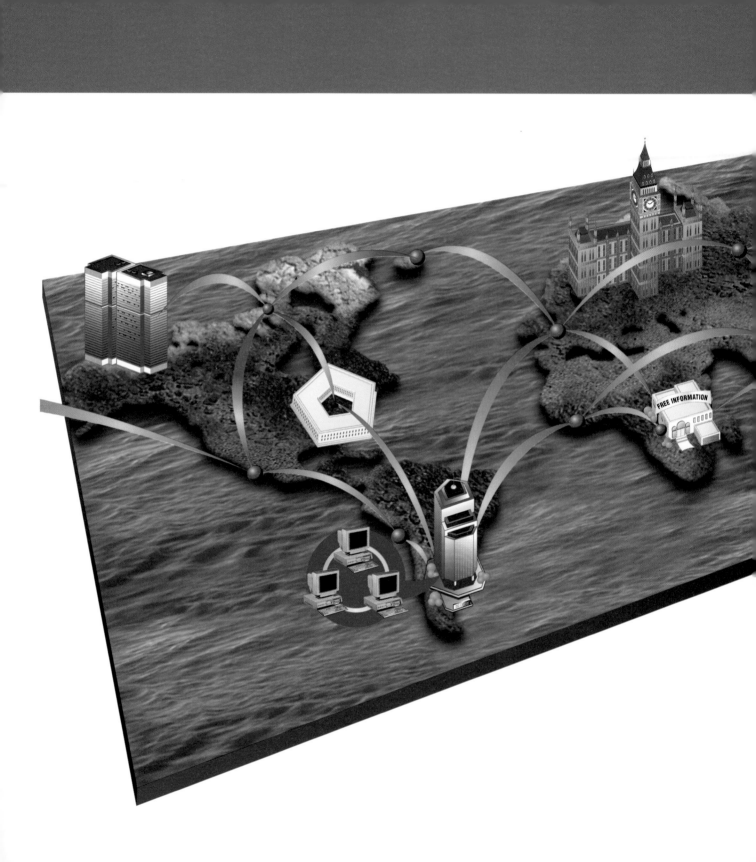

CHAPTER 10

The Internet

What is the Internet and how can I get connected? This chapter will help you start exploring the Internet.

INTRODUCTION TO THE INTERNET

The Internet is the largest computer network in the world.

In the late 1960s, the U.S. Defense Department began the Internet. The network quickly grew to include scientists and researchers across the country and eventually included schools, businesses, libraries and individuals around the world.

The Internet consists of thousands of connected networks around the world. A network is a collection of computers that are connected to share information. Each government, company and organization on the Internet is responsible for maintaining its own network.

If part of the Internet fails, information finds a new route around the disabled computers.

Most of the information on the Internet is free. Governments, universities, colleges, companies and individuals provide free information to educate and entertain the public.

FREE INFORMATION

The Internet is often called the Net, the Information Superhighway or Cyberspace.

WHAT THE INTERNET OFFERS

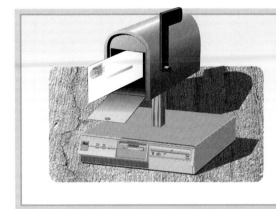

Electronic Mail

Exchanging electronic mail (e-mail) is the most popular feature on the Internet. You can exchange electronic mail with people around the world, including friends, colleagues, family members, customers and even people you meet on the Internet. Electronic mail is fast, easy, inexpensive and saves paper.

Information

The Internet gives you access to information on any subject imaginable. You can review newspapers, magazines, academic papers, government documents, television show transcripts, famous speeches, recipes, job listings, works by Shakespeare, airline schedules and much more.

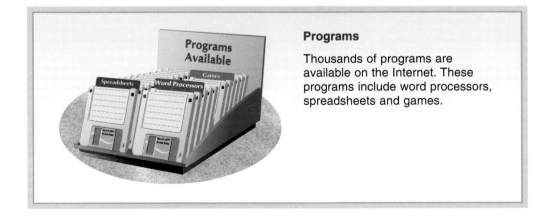

Programs

Thousands of programs are available on the Internet. These programs include word processors, spreadsheets and games.

Entertainment

Hundreds of simple games are available free of charge on the Internet, including backgammon, chess, poker and football.

On the Internet, you can review current movies, listen to television theme songs, read movie scripts and have interactive conversations with people around the world—even celebrities.

Newsgroups

You can join newsgroups, also called discussion groups, on the Internet to meet people around the world with similar interests. You can ask questions, discuss problems and read interesting stories.

There are thousands of newsgroups on topics such as the environment, food, humor, music, pets, photography, politics, religion, sports and television.

Online Shopping

You can order goods and services on the Internet without leaving your desk. You can buy items such as books, computer programs, flowers, music CDs, pizza, stocks and used cars.

HOW INFORMATION TRANSFERS

All computers on the
Internet work together
to transfer information
around the world.

Packets

When you send information over
the Internet, the information is broken
down into smaller pieces, called packets.
Each packet travels independently over
the Internet and may take a different path
to arrive at the intended destination.

When information arrives at its
destination, the packets are reassembled.

The Future of the Internet

Several organizations are currently
developing faster ways of transferring
information over the Internet.

Internet2 (I2) will enhance the transfer
of information between universities
and research facilities in the United
States. Project Oxygen, also called
the Super-Internet, plans to improve
the transfer of complex information,
such as video, on the Internet.

TCP/IP

Transmission Control Protocol/Internet
Protocol (TCP/IP) is a language computers
on the Internet use to communicate with
each other. TCP/IP divides information you
send into packets and sends the packets
over the Internet. When information arrives
at the intended destination, TCP/IP ensures
that all the packets arrived safely.

Router

A router is a specialized computer that regulates traffic on the Internet and picks the most efficient route for each packet. A packet may pass through many routers before reaching its intended destination.

Backbone

The backbone of the Internet consists of high-speed data lines that connect major networks all over the world.

Download/Upload Information

When you receive information from another computer on the Internet, you are downloading the information.

When you send information to another computer on the Internet, you are uploading the information.

GETTING CONNECTED

You need specific equipment and programs to connect to the Internet.

Computer

You can use any type of computer, such as an IBM-compatible or Macintosh computer, to connect to the Internet.

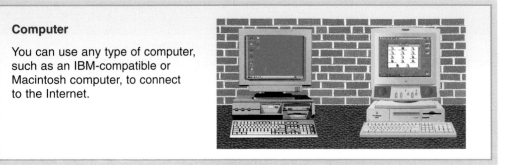

Programs

You need special programs to use the Internet. Most companies that connect you to the Internet provide the programs you need free of charge.

Modem

You need a modem to connect to the Internet. You should choose at least a 33.6 Kbps modem, although a 56 Kbps modem is recommended. For more information about modems, see page 50.

INTERNET SERVICE PROVIDER

An Internet Service Provider (ISP) is a company that gives you access to the Internet for a fee.

Cost

Many Internet service providers offer you a certain number of hours per day or month for a set fee. If you exceed the total number of hours, you are usually charged for every extra hour you use the provider.

Some providers offer unlimited access to the Internet for a set fee. Make sure you are aware of any hidden charges or restrictions.

COMMERCIAL ONLINE SERVICE

A commercial online service is a company that offers a vast amount of information and access to the Internet for a fee.

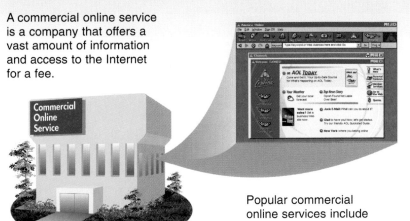

Popular commercial online services include America Online and The Microsoft Network.

Cost

Most commercial online services let you try their service free of charge for a limited time. After the trial period, most online services offer a certain number of hours per day or month for a set fee. If you exceed the total number of hours, you are usually charged for every extra hour you use the online service.

Some online services offer unlimited access to the service and the Internet for a set fee.

CHAPTER 11

The World Wide Web

What is the World Wide Web? This chapter introduces you to the Web and what it has to offer.

INTRODUCTION TO THE WEB

The World Wide Web is part of the Internet. The Web consists of a huge collection of documents stored on computers around the world.

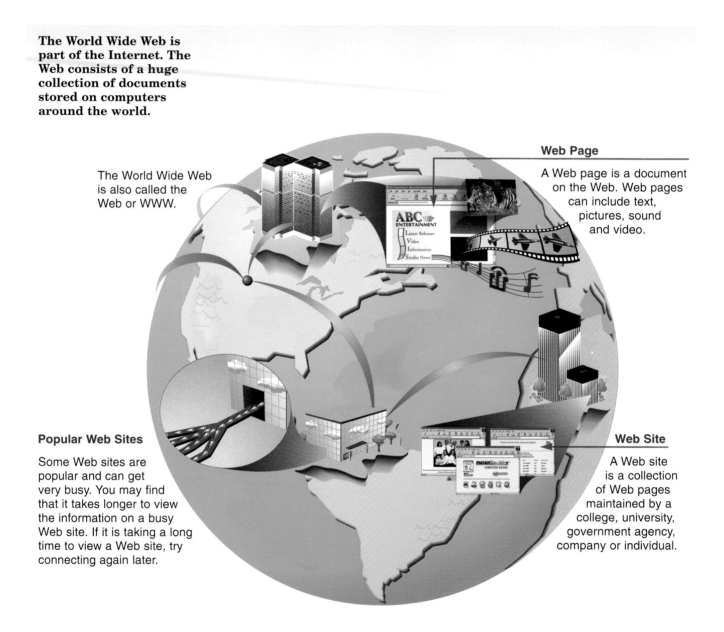

The World Wide Web is also called the Web or WWW.

Web Page

A Web page is a document on the Web. Web pages can include text, pictures, sound and video.

Popular Web Sites

Some Web sites are popular and can get very busy. You may find that it takes longer to view the information on a busy Web site. If it is taking a long time to view a Web site, try connecting again later.

Web Site

A Web site is a collection of Web pages maintained by a college, university, government agency, company or individual.

URL

Each Web page has a unique address, called the Uniform Resource Locator (URL). You can instantly display any Web page if you know its URL.

■ All Web page URLs start with http (HyperText Transfer Protocol).

HYPERTEXT

Web pages are hypertext documents. A hypertext document contains highlighted text that connects to other pages on the Web. You can easily jump from one Web page to another by selecting the highlighted text.

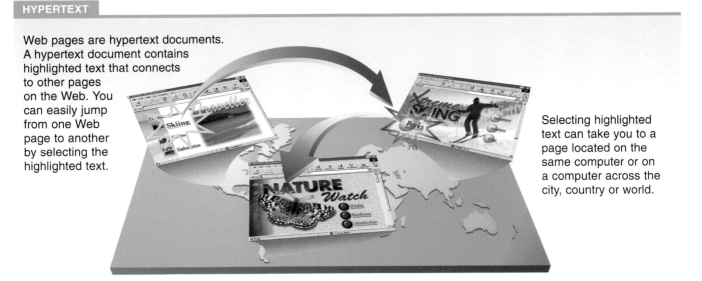

Selecting highlighted text can take you to a page located on the same computer or on a computer across the city, country or world.

A Web browser is a program that lets you view and explore information on the Web.

WEB BROWSER SCREEN

Most Web browsers have a similar look and feel.

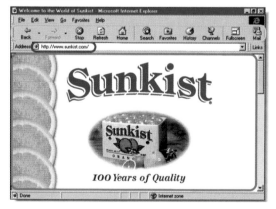

■ This area displays the address of the page you are currently viewing.

■ This area displays a Web page.

■ This area displays a toolbar to help you quickly perform common tasks.

HOME PAGE

The home page is the page that appears each time you start your Web browser.

You can choose any page on the Web as your home page. Make sure you choose a home page that provides a good starting point for exploring the Web.

Bookmarks

Most Web browsers have a feature called bookmarks or favorites. This feature lets you store the addresses of Web pages you frequently visit. Bookmarks save you from having to remember and constantly retype your favorite Web page addresses.

History List

When you are browsing through pages on the World Wide Web, it can be difficult to keep track of the locations of pages you have visited. Most Web browsers include a history list that allows you to quickly return to any Web page you have recently visited.

Turn Off Images

Images, or pictures, may take a while to appear on your screen. You can save time by turning off the display of images. When you turn off the display of images, an icon (example: 🖼️) will appear in place of any images.

Images On   Images Off

INTERNET EXPLORER

Internet Explorer is a popular Web browser from Microsoft.

The latest version of Internet Explorer includes additional programs that you can use to access and exchange information on the Internet.

You can get the latest version of Internet Explorer at the following Web site:

www.microsoft.com

Browse the Web

Internet Explorer integrates the World Wide Web, your corporate network and your Windows 95 or 98 desktop so you can browse through information more efficiently. Internet Explorer also provides enhanced security features so you can safely purchase items on the Internet.

Exchange Electronic Mail

Internet Explorer includes Outlook Express, which enables you to exchange e-mail messages with people around the world. Outlook Express allows you to enhance your messages with images, animation and multimedia.

Participate in Newsgroups

You can use Internet Explorer's Outlook Express to join discussion groups, called newsgroups, to meet people around the world with similar interests. There are thousands of newsgroups on many different topics.

Create Web Pages

Internet Explorer includes FrontPage Express, which allows you to create and edit your own Web pages. You can place pages you create on the Web so people around the world can view your information.

Participate in Conferences

Internet Explorer includes NetMeeting, which allows you to easily communicate with another person on the Internet. You can chat with a colleague, exchange files and work together on the same document.

View Channels

Internet Explorer lets you view channels of information. A channel is a Web site that automatically delivers information to your computer at times you specify. Any Web site can be a channel. You can have channels that cover topics such as home decorating, movies, music, news, stocks or travel.

Multimedia is an effective way of attracting attention to information on a Web page.

Many companies that advertise on the Web use multimedia–a combination of text, images, sound and video or animation–to sell their products and services.

TEXT AND IMAGES

You can view documents on the Web, such as newspapers, magazines, plays and famous speeches. You can also view images on the Web, such as pictures of celebrities and famous paintings. Most Web pages contain a combination of text and images.

SOUND AND VIDEO

You can listen to sound on the Web, such as TV theme songs, movie soundtracks and historical speeches.

You can also view video on the Web, such as news or movie clips, cartoons and interviews with celebrities.

STREAMING MULTIMEDIA

Streaming multimedia is a system that lets you hear or view continuous sound or video on the Web, such as a live concert or sporting event.

Most Web browsers cannot automatically play streaming multimedia. You must get a program such as RealNetworks RealPlayer or Microsoft NetShow to play streaming multimedia on the Web.

WEB PAGE ENHANCEMENTS

Most new Web browsers can display Java, JavaScript and ActiveX enhancements.

Java

Java is a complex programming language that allows people to create animated and interactive Web pages. Java-enhanced Web pages can display animation and moving text, play music and much more.

JavaScript

JavaScript is a simple programming language that is used mainly for Web page enhancements, such as displaying scrolling messages and fading-in Web pages.

ActiveX

ActiveX is a technology used to improve Web pages. For example, people can use ActiveX to add pop-up menus that instantly display a list of options on a Web page.

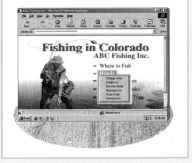

SHOPPING ON THE WEB

You can buy products and services on the Web without ever leaving your desk.

There are thousands of products you can buy on the Web, such as clothing, flowers, office supplies and computer programs.

The Web also offers a range of services, such as banking, financial and real estate advice.

COMPANIES

Many companies allow you to view and buy their products on the Web.

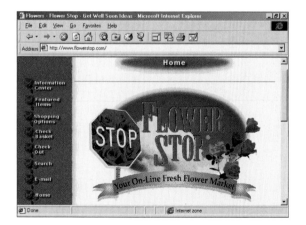

You can view a list of companies on the Web at:

www.bizweb.com

SHOPPING MALLS

There are shopping malls on the Web where you can view and buy products and services offered by many different companies.

You can view a list of shopping malls on the Web at:

www.nsns.com/MouseTracks/HallofMalls.html

Security is important when you want to send personal information, such as credit card numbers, over the Internet.

SECURE WEB PAGES

There are secure pages on the Web that protect confidential information sent over the Internet. Secure Web pages work with Web browsers to create an almost unbreakable security system.

Sending a credit card number to a secure Web page can be safer than giving the credit card number to an unknown person over the phone.

VISIT A SECURE WEB PAGE

The address of a secure Web page usually starts with https rather than http. When you visit a secure Web page, your Web browser will usually display a lock on the screen to indicate that the Web page is secure.

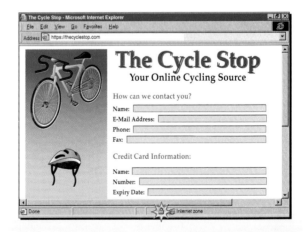

SEARCH THE WEB

There are many free services you can use to find information on the Web. These services are called search tools.

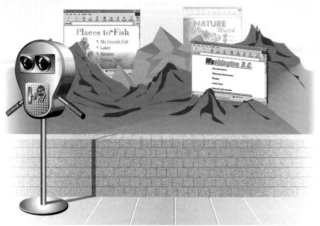

A search tool catalogs Web pages to make them easier to find. Some search tools record every word on a Web page, while others record only the name of each page.

HOW SEARCH TOOLS FIND WEB PAGES

There are two ways search tools find pages on the Web. Since hundreds of new pages are created each day, it is impossible for search tools to catalog every new page on the Web.

Robots

Most search tools have automated robots that travel around the Web looking for new pages.

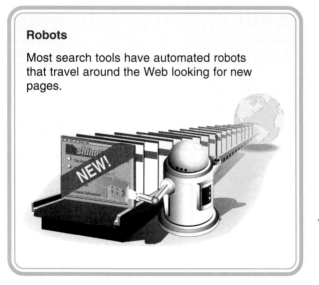

Submissions

People often submit information about Web pages they have created.

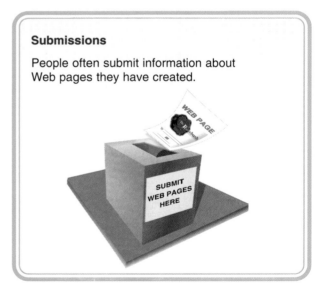

Browse Through Categories

You can browse through categories such as arts, science or sports to find information that interests you. When you select a category of interest, a list of subcategories appears. You can continue to select subcategories until you find a Web page that interests you.

Search by Topic

You can type a word into a search tool to find a specific topic that interests you. The search tool will display a list of pages containing the word you specified.

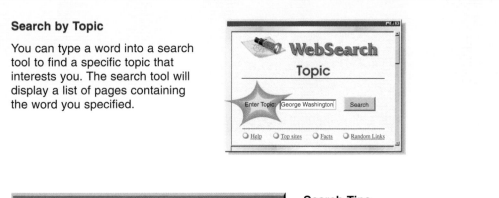

"Chicago Bears"	Find Web pages containing these words in this exact sequence
+painting -watercolor	Find Web pages containing "painting" but not "watercolor"
Tom OR Thomas	Find Web pages containing one of these words

Search Tips

When searching by topic, most search tools allow you to make your search more precise. For example, you may be able to search for a specific group of words by typing quotation marks around the group of words you want to find. Many search tools also allow you to make your search more precise by typing a special command or symbol.

A Web portal is a Web site that provides an excellent starting point for exploring the Internet.

Web portals let you type a word or phrase to quickly search for information on the Web. Web portals also allow you to browse through categories, such as business or sports, to find information that interests you.

POPULAR WEB PORTALS

There are several popular Web portals you can use.

Excite

www.excite.com

Netscape Netcenter

www.netscape.com

Yahoo!

www.yahoo.com

E-mail

Web portals usually offer free e-mail services, which allow you to send and receive e-mail from any computer that has access to the Web.

News

Most Web portals provide a variety of up-to-date news headlines, as well as sports scores and stock quotes. You can select a news headline to read a full article on the news item. Some Web portals also provide video and audio clips for news items.

Chat

Web portals often offer chat services that allow you to instantly communicate with people around the world.

Customize

You can customize many Web portals to display the information you want. For example, you could customize a Web portal to display the weather forecast for your area.

CHILDREN AND THE WEB

Children should be carefully monitored when browsing the World Wide Web.

Most of the information on the Web is meant to educate or entertain readers, but some sites may contain material you find inappropriate.

TYPES OF INAPPROPRIATE INFORMATION

Pictures

There are many sites on the Web that display pictures meant for adult users. Most adult-oriented sites require verification that users are adults, but the sites often display sample pictures on the first page of the Web site.

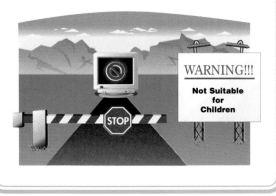

Documents

There are many documents on the Web describing everything from causing mischief at school to making explosives. These types of documents may appeal to teenagers and are usually found at Web sites distributing banned or censored books. These Web sites generally do not have any restrictions on who can access the documents.

HOW TO RESTRICT ACCESS

Adult Supervision

Constant adult supervision is the best way to ensure that children do not access inappropriate information on the Web.

Before each Web browsing session, the adult and child should decide on the purpose of the session, such as researching a school project. This will help set ground rules for browsing and make the time spent on the Web more productive.

Browser Restrictions

Some Web browsers allow you to restrict the information children can access on the Web. Many Web sites are rated using a system similar to the one used to rate television shows and films.

You can set your Web browser to allow access only to Web sites that comply with specific ratings.

Restriction Programs

You can buy programs that let you restrict access to certain Web sites. Most of these programs provide a frequently updated list of Web sites considered inappropriate for children.

You can purchase restriction programs at the following Web sites:

Cyber Patrol
www.cyberpatrol.com

Net Nanny
www.netnanny.com

CREATE AND PUBLISH WEB PAGES

You can create and publish pages on the World Wide Web to share information with people around the world.

Individuals publish Web pages to share their favorite pictures, hobbies and interests. Companies publish Web pages to promote their businesses, advertise products and publicize job openings.

Organize Ideas

Before you start creating Web pages, decide what ideas you will discuss and how the ideas relate to one another. Break up your information so you discuss only one major idea on each page. You may find it helpful to first sketch the design of your pages on paper.

HTML

HyperText Markup Language (HTML) is a computer code used to create Web pages. There are many programs available, called HTML editors, which can help you create Web pages without learning HTML. Popular HTML editors include Microsoft's FrontPage and Sausage Software's HotDog Pro.

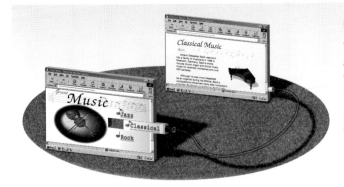

Links

You can add links to your Web pages. A link allows readers to select an image or highlighted text to display another page on the Web. Links are one of the most important features of your Web pages since they let readers move easily through information of interest.

Images

You can add images to your Web pages to make the pages more attractive. You can create these images on your computer, copy them from the Web or use a scanner to copy them from printed material. When using images that are not your own, be aware of copyright restrictions.

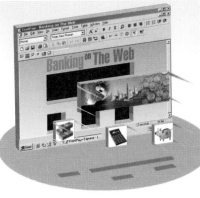

Avoid placing a large number of images on your Web pages. Images increase the time it takes for Web pages to appear on the screen.

Publish Your Web Pages

When you finish creating your Web pages, you can publish the pages by transferring them to a Web server. The company that gives you access to the Internet usually offers space on its Web server where you can publish your Web pages.

CHAPTER 12

Interesting Web Sites

Feeling overwhelmed by the amount of information on the Web? This chapter describes 80 interesting sites and provides a good place to start your Web exploration.

ARTS AND ENTERTAINMENT

Hollywood Online

Great news, video clips of upcoming films and interviews with your favorite stars.

 www.hollywood.com

Internet Movie Database

This free source of movie information is the largest of its kind on the Internet.

 www.us.imdb.com

Louvre Museum

A huge collection of some of the world's best art.

 www.culture.fr/louvre

Mr. Showbiz

Articles, reviews, the latest news from the entertainment world and much more.

 www.mrshowbiz.com

People Online

Get the scoop on your favorite celebrities at People Online. This Web site includes features on the biggest names in show business.

URL www.people.com

Theatre Central

Your one-stop guide to theatre on the Internet, complete with job listings, professional contacts and links to other theatre-related sites.

URL www.theatre-central.com

TV Guide Entertainment Network

This online guide provides the latest TV news and gossip, as well as local program listings.

URL www.tvgen.com

World Wide Arts Resources

Are you looking for specific art information? Check out this complete guide to art and culture on the Web.

URL www.wwar.com

American Express

Locate American Express offices around the world, book your next trip, check your bill, explore the Small Business Exchange, apply for a card and more at this site.

 www.americanexpress.com

American Stock Exchange

Check today's market summary or look back through the past year's archives.

URL www.amex.com

Bloomberg Website

Business buffs can stay on top of the latest business news and stock market figures by visiting this Web site.

URL www.bloomberg.com

CareerMosaic

Many of the world's largest corporations post open job positions at this site.

URL www.careermosaic.com

CNNfn

A great source for business news and special reports from around the globe.

URL www.cnnfn.com

E*TRADE

Trade stocks over the Internet, get stock quotes or play the E*TRADE Stock Market Trading Game.

URL www.etrade.com

Fortune

A collection of the latest in-depth business features Fortune Magazine is famous for, as well as daily online business reports.

URL www.fortune.com

Silicon Investor

Thinking of investing in the stock market? This popular bulletin board service allows you to discuss business trends with investors and business professionals from around the world.

URL www.siliconinvestor.com

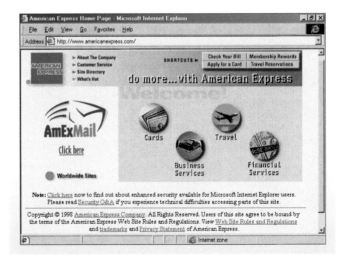

FOOD AND DRINK

Food Channel

A great starting point for food information, whether you are searching for industry trends, food fun, dining out advice, cooking help or anything else.

 www.foodchannel.com

Godiva Chocolatier

Some of the best and most exotic chocolate recipes in the world are available here, complete with mouth-watering pictures.

 www.godiva.com

Kellogg's

Jump into the Cereal City Headquarters! Flip through the cookbook or play some games in the Clubhouse.

 www.kelloggs.com

Milk

Tickle your taste buds with all the delicious recipes that include milk! Ask the personal trainer how best to include milk in your diet.

URL www.whymilk.com

Ragu

This is a top-notch site with recipes, contests and guides to speaking Italian.

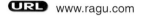 www.ragu.com

Star Chefs

Interviews, biographies and recipes from some of the world's top chefs.

 www.starchefs.com

Sunkist

Quench your thirst for information about citrus at this site that also offers interesting recipes and nutrition facts!

 www.sunkist.com

Veggies Unite!

A great collection of vegetarian recipes and cooking tips, a veggie glossary and more.

 www.vegweb.com

Ask Dr. Science

Scientific proof that scientists have a sense of humor too. Check out Dr. Science's answer to the question of the day.

 www.drscience.com

Center for the Easily Amused

This monster list of humorous sites on the Web is a comedy fan's dream come true.

 www.amused.com

Comedy Central Online

Visit the site of this television comedy channel for a few laughs.

 www.comcentral.com

Comics

Find all your favorite newspaper comic strips at this site.

 www.ctoons.com

Fade to Black

A comedy magazine with biting wit and cyber know-how.

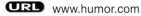 www.fadetoblack.com

Humor.com

Check out extensive pictures and bios of world-famous comedians, link to your favorite comic strips or visit the joke database.

 www.humor.com

Jokes.com

Read the cartoons, see the joke of the day or submit a joke of your own!

URL www.jokes.com

Rec.humor.funny Home Page

Thousands of jokes and humorous stories make this site a popular hangout for cyber-comedians.

URL www.netfunny.com

CNET: The Computer Network

Find out what's coming up next week on this acclaimed cable computer news show or review the transcript from a previous episode.

 www.cnet.com/Content/Tv

CNN Interactive

Read the latest headlines, try today's quiz or visit the Video Vault to watch video clips of recent news.

 www.cnn.com

Electronic Newsstand

Browse through many popular magazines and even subscribe to your favorites online.

 www.enews.com

Financial Times

This site makes it easy to follow the world's business, economic and political news.

 www.usa.ft.com

NewsPage

Need up-to-date information about a specific industry? Find news on everything from computers to health care at this site.

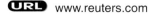 www.newspage.com

Reuters

A major source of financial and business information. Visit the source where many publishers, broadcasters and online services get their news.

 www.reuters.com

The New York Times

Get your daily helping of local, national and international news stories from this online newspaper.

 www.nytimes.com

USA Today

The online version of one of the most popular American national newspapers.

www.usatoday.com

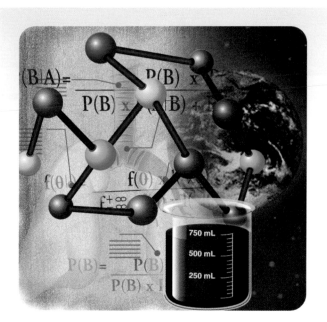

American Chemical Society (ACSWeb)

Discover information about this society, articles from chemical journals, a software catalog and more.

 www.acs.org

Daily Planet

This site offers information about weather and includes an online guide to meteorology.

 www.atmos.uiuc.edu

National Library of Medicine

Access medical and scientific information from this huge library.

 www.nlm.nih.gov

National Space Science Data Center

This site contains a collection of images from space, complete with informative descriptions.

URL http://nssdc.gsfc.nasa.gov

Popular Science

This science magazine brings you the latest innovations in technology and allows you to test your scientific knowledge with games and trivia questions.

 www.popularscience.com

Science Daily

Your link to the latest in scientific discovery from universities and research organizations around the globe.

URL www.sciencedaily.com

Science Online

Find out about interesting new developments in research and gain free access to science forums, news and career resources.

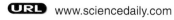 www.sciencemag.org

United States Environmental Protection Agency

Become more environmentally aware at this site which provides everything from teaching aids and gardening tips to the latest environmental news.

URL www.epa.gov

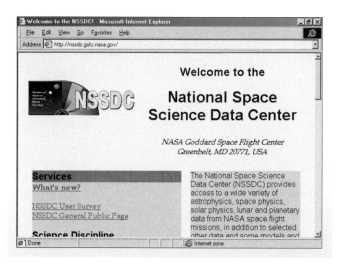

SEARCH TOOLS

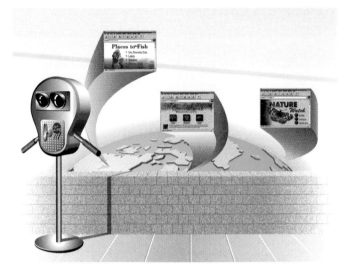

AltaVista

Quickly search millions of Web pages and thousands of newsgroups.

 www.altavista.digital.com

Deja News

Calling itself the premier Usenet search utility, Deja News lets you perform simple or detailed searches of all newsgroups.

URL www.dejanews.com

Four11

Looking for someone on the Internet? Visit Four11 and access over 6.5 million e-mail addresses.

URL www.four11.com

HotBot

Get connected with this award-winning search engine, brought to you by Wired magazine.

 www.hotbot.com

Infoseek

A diverse search tool that lets you search the Web, newsgroups or e-mail addresses.

 www.infoseek.com

Lycos

Search the Web or check out the directory service from Carnegie Mellon University.

URL www.lycos.com

Search.com

This site combines hundreds of search tools to help you find anything and everything you need.

 www.search.com

Yahoo!

The first popular search tool, Yahoo! provides a colorful guide to the online world.

URL www.yahoo.com

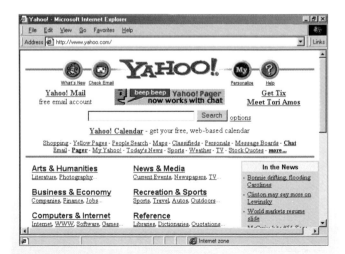

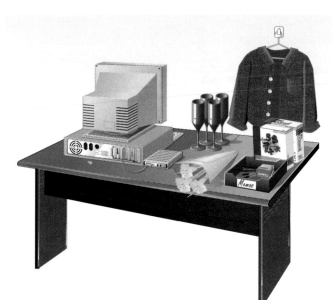

Amazon.com

Navigate through reviews, excerpts and articles while you shop for the latest in books and music at this comprehensive site.

 www.amazon.com

Bloomingdales

With thousands of products available online, this is a great place to find anything you need. Search for a product by department or by your favorite designer.

 www.bloomingdales.com

CD NOW

Find everything from Abba to Zappa and the latest chart topping hits at the Internet's number one music store.

 www.cdnow.com

Dell

Technical support, a virtual computer store, even live broadcasts of shareholders meetings are all just a mouse click away at this company site.

 www.dell.com

Neiman Marcus

If you wish to have a personal shopper do your shopping, this site is for you. Order anything from a perfect gift to a new outfit.

 www.neimanmarcus.com

Spiegel

You name it, they've got it—electronics, clothing, home furnishings and more!

 www.spiegel.com

The Gap

Find out what's hot in fashion for the whole family. You can even get dressed online by mixing and matching the latest clothing on a model!

 www.gap.com

Wal-Mart

Purchase Wal-Mart products online!

 www.wal-mart.com

ESPN SportsZone

The latest in sports from ESPN, with feature articles, statistics and scores.

 www.espn.sportszone.com

golf.com

A top-notch golf site with professional and amateur golf coverage alongside information on golf equipment, schools, resorts and major golf publications.

 www.golf.com

NBA.com

The official site for the National Basketball Association.

 www.nba.com

NFL.com

The home page of the National Football League.

 www.nfl.com

NHL.com

Schedules, news, scores, teams, superstars and more from the National Hockey League's official Web site.

 www.nhl.com

Sports Illustrated Online

This site offers sports stories and a sampling of the famous Swimsuit Issue.

www.pathfinder.com/si

The Official Site of Major League Baseball

All the latest scores! All the latest news! The home page for Major League Baseball.

www.majorleaguebaseball.com

The Sports Network

Check out TSN's Web site to find coverage of many sports.

www.sportsnetwork.com

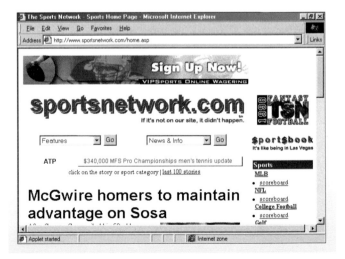

Excite Travel

This site offers links to information about thousands of destinations around the world.

 www.city.net

Family Travel Forum

A great tool for people planning to travel with their kids. This site offers useful advice and great deals.

 www.familytravelforum.com

Internet Cruise Travel Network

A great guide for anyone interested in cruises, with information on everything from day cruises to ocean freighters.

 www.cruisetravel.com

Mapquest

This site offers helpful information on hotels and attractions that will help you plan the perfect getaway. It even includes driving directions!

 www.mapquest.com

Online Vacation Mall

Find a perfect vacation—you can book or cancel your reservations online.

 www.onlinevacationmall.com

Preview Travel

Get away from it all! This site offers you all the tools to plan the perfect vacation that is right for you.

 www.previewtravel.com

TravelWeb

Choose from thousands of hotels around the world and make a reservation online.

 www.travelweb.com

Vacation.com

From whitewater rafting to safaris, bicycle trips to cruises, this is the place to go if you're looking for a fun and active vacation.

 www.vacation.com

CHAPTER 13

Electronic Mail

How can I communicate with other people on the Internet? This chapter introduces you to electronic mail.

INTRODUCTION TO E-MAIL

You can exchange electronic mail (e-mail) with people around the world.

E-mail is a convenient way to communicate with family, friends and colleagues.

E-MAIL PROGRAM

An e-mail program lets you send, receive and manage your e-mail messages.

Popular e-mail programs include Microsoft Outlook Express and Qualcomm Eudora Pro.

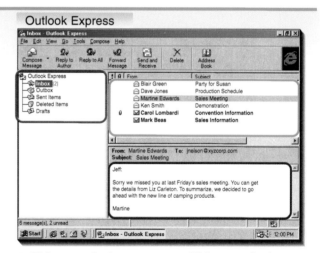

Outlook Express

■ This area displays the folders that contain your e-mail messages.

■ This area displays a list of all your e-mail messages.

■ This area displays the contents of a single e-mail message.

Speed

E-mail is much faster than old-fashioned mail, called "snail mail." An e-mail message can travel around the world in minutes.

Cost

Once you pay a service provider for a connection to the Internet, there is no charge for sending and receiving e-mail. You do not have to pay extra even if you send a long message or the message travels around the world.

Exchanging e-mail can save you money on long distance calls. The next time you are about to pick up the telephone, consider sending an e-mail message instead.

Convenience

You can create and send e-mail messages at any time. Unlike telephone calls, the person receiving the message does not have to be at the computer when you send the message. E-mail makes communicating with people in different time zones very convenient.

You can send a message to anyone around the world if you know the person's e-mail address.

An e-mail address defines the location of an individual's mailbox on the Internet.

PARTS OF AN E-MAIL ADDRESS

An e-mail address consists of two parts separated by the @ ("at") symbol. An e-mail address cannot contain spaces.

mvickers@sales.abc.com

■ The **user name** is the name of the person's account. This can be a real name or a nickname.

■ The domain name is the location of the person's account on the Internet. Periods (.) separate the various parts of the domain name.

FAMOUS E-MAIL ADDRESSES

NAME	ADDRESS
Bill Gates	billg@microsoft.com
Brad Pitt	ciaobox@msn.com
Madonna	Madonna@wbr.com
President	president@whitehouse.gov
Tom Brokaw	nightly@nbc.com
Tom Clancy	tomclancy@aol.com

ORGANIZATION OR COUNTRY

The last few characters in an e-mail address usually indicate the type of organization or the country the person belongs to.

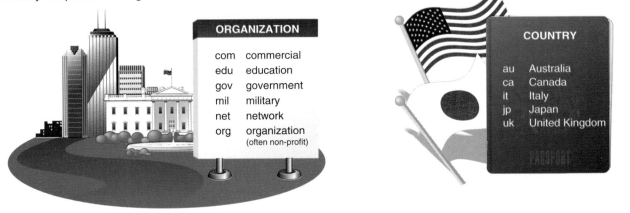

ORGANIZATION

com	commercial
edu	education
gov	government
mil	military
net	network
org	organization (often non-profit)

COUNTRY

au	Australia
ca	Canada
it	Italy
jp	Japan
uk	United Kingdom

BOUNCED MESSAGES

A bounced message is a message that returns to you because it cannot reach its destination. A message usually bounces because of typing mistakes in the e-mail address.

Before sending a message, make sure you check the e-mail address for accuracy.

SEND A MESSAGE

You can send a message to exchange ideas or request information.

When you send a message, do not assume the person will read the message right away. Some people may not regularly check their messages.

If you want to practice sending a message, send a message to yourself.

Writing Style

Make sure every message you send is clear, concise and contains no spelling or grammar errors. Also make sure the message will not be misinterpreted. For example, the reader may not realize a statement is meant to be sarcastic.

Signature

You can have an e-mail program add information about yourself to the end of every message you send. This prevents you from having to type the same information over and over again. You can also use plain characters to display simple pictures.

Smileys

You can use special characters, called smileys or emoticons, to express emotions in messages. These characters resemble human faces if you turn them sideways.

SMILEYS

Gesture	Characters
Cry	:'-(
Frown	:-(
Indifferent	:-I
Laugh	:-D
Smile	:-)
Surprise	:-0
Wink	;-)

Abbreviations

Abbreviations are commonly used in messages to save time typing.

Abbreviation	Meaning	Abbreviation	Meaning
BTW	by the way	LOL	laughing out loud
FAQ	frequently asked questions	MOTAS	member of the appropriate sex
FOAF	friend of a friend	MOTOS	member of the opposite sex
FWIW	for what it's worth		
FYI	for your information	MOTSS	member of the same sex
IMHO	in my humble opinion		
IMO	in my opinion	ROTFL	rolling on the floor laughing
IOW	in other words	SO	significant other
L8R	later	WRT	with respect to

Shouting

A MESSAGE WRITTEN IN CAPITAL LETTERS IS ANNOYING AND HARD TO READ. THIS IS CALLED SHOUTING.

Always use upper and lower case letters when typing messages.

Flame

A flame is an angry or insulting message directed at one person. A flame war is an argument that continues for a while. Avoid starting or participating in flame wars.

E-MAIL FEATURES

RECEIVE A MESSAGE

You do not have to be at your computer to receive a message. Your service provider keeps all your messages until you retrieve them. Make sure you regularly check for messages.

You can use a computer with a modem to connect to your service provider and retrieve messages. This allows you to check your messages while traveling.

REPLY TO A MESSAGE

You can reply to a message to answer a question, express an opinion or supply additional information.

When you reply to a message, make sure you include part of the original message. This is called quoting. Quoting helps the reader identify which message you are replying to. To save the reader time, make sure you delete all parts of the original message that do not directly relate to your reply.

ATTACH A FILE TO A MESSAGE

You can attach a document, picture, sound, video or program to a message you are sending.

You should keep the size of an attached file under 150 kilobytes. Many computers on the Internet have trouble transferring large attached files.

The computer receiving the message must have a program that can view or play the attached file.

FORWARD A MESSAGE

After reading a message, you can add comments and then send the message to a friend or colleague.

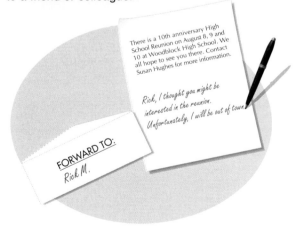

PRINT A MESSAGE

You can print a message to produce a paper copy of the message.

CHAPTER 14

Mailing Lists

What are mailing lists and how do they work? This chapter introduces you to mailing lists and provides helpful tips on how to join them.

INTRODUCTION TO MAILING LISTS

A mailing list is a discussion group that uses e-mail to communicate.

There are thousands of mailing lists that cover a wide variety of topics, from aromatherapy to Led Zeppelin. New mailing lists are created every week.

HOW MAILING LISTS WORK

When a mailing list receives a message, a copy of the message goes to everyone on the mailing list.

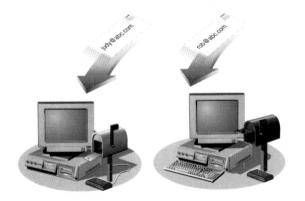

Most mailing lists let you send and receive messages. Many mailing lists only let you receive messages, not send them.

FIND MAILING LISTS

You can find a list of mailing lists at the following Web site:

www.neosoft.com/internet/paml

You can search for mailing lists that discuss a specific topic at the following Web site:

www.liszt.com

A Word A Day

Sends you a word and its definition every day.
Contact: wsmith@wordsmith.org
Type in subject line: subscribe Your Name

Golf Discussion List

Discussion of the game of golf.
Contact:
listserv@LISTSERV.ACSU.BUFFALO.EDU
Type in message: subscribe golf-l

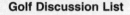

Choco

Sends you a collection of chocolate recipes once a month.
Contact: majordomo@apk.net
Type in message: subscribe choco

Joke A Day

Sends you a joke six days a week.
Contact: join@jokeaday.com

Dinosaur

Discussion of dinosaurs and other prehistoric animals.
Contact: listproc@usc.edu
Type in message: SUBSCRIBE DINOSAUR Your Name

Railroad

Discussion of real and model railroads.
Contact: listserv@CUNYVM.CUNY.EDU
Type in message: subscribe railroad

Gardens

Discussion of home gardening.
Contact: listserv@LSV.UKY.EDU
Type in message: subscribe gardens

X-Files

Discussion of the popular television series.
Contact: listproc@lists.pipex.com
Type in message: subscribe x-files Your Name

SUBSCRIBE TO A MAILING LIST

Just as you would subscribe to a newspaper or magazine, you can subscribe to a mailing list that interests you.

Subscribing adds your e-mail address to the mailing list.

Unsubscribe

If you no longer want to receive messages from a mailing list, you can unsubscribe from the mailing list at any time. Unsubscribing removes your e-mail address from the mailing list.

MAILING LIST ADDRESSES

Each mailing list has two addresses. Make sure you send your messages to the appropriate address.

Mailing List Address

The mailing list address receives messages intended for the entire mailing list. This is the address you use to send messages you want all the people on the list to receive. Do not send subscription or unsubscription requests to the mailing list address.

Administrative Address

The administrative address receives messages dealing with administrative issues. This is the address you use to subscribe to or unsubscribe from a mailing list.

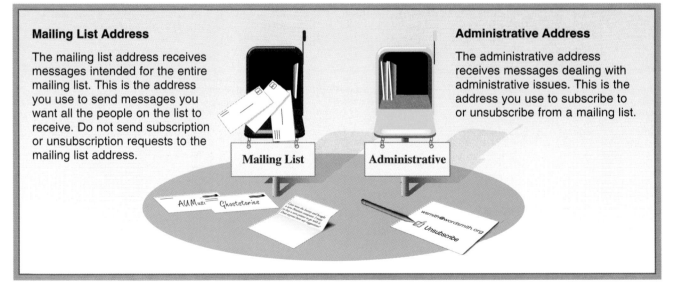

Welcome Message

When you subscribe to a mailing list, you usually receive a welcome message to confirm that your e-mail address has been added to the list. This message may explain any rules the mailing list has about sending messages to the list.

Check for Messages

After you subscribe to a mailing list, make sure you check your mailbox frequently. You can receive dozens of messages in a short period of time.

Digests

If you receive a lot of messages from a mailing list, find out if the list is available as a digest. A digest groups individual messages together and sends them to you as one message.

Vacations

When you go on vacation, make sure you temporarily unsubscribe from all your mailing lists. This will prevent your mailbox from overflowing with messages.

TYPES OF MAILING LISTS

MANUALLY MAINTAINED LISTS

A person manages a manually maintained mailing list.

A manually maintained list may contain the word "request" in its e-mail address (example: american-revolution-l-request@rootsweb.com).

Join a List

When you want to join a manually maintained list, make sure you find out what information the administrator needs and include the information in your message.

AUTOMATED LISTS

A computer program manages an automated mailing list. There are three popular programs that manage automated lists–listproc, listserv and majordomo.

An automated list typically contains the name of the program that manages the list in its e-mail address (example: majordomo@apk.net).

Join a List

When you want to join an automated list, make sure you find out what information the program needs and include the information in your message. If a program does not understand your message, it may not respond to your request.

PRIVATE MAILING LISTS

Most mailing lists allow anyone with an e-mail address to subscribe, but some mailing lists restrict membership to a specific group of people. For example, a mailing list about surgery may be restricted to doctors.

For private mailing lists, you may need to answer a questionnaire. A volunteer reads the questionnaire and decides if you have the qualifications required to join the list.

MODERATED MAILING LISTS

Some mailing lists are moderated. A volunteer reads each message sent to a moderated list and decides if the message is appropriate for the list. If the message is appropriate, the volunteer sends the message to every person on the mailing list.

A moderated mailing list keeps discussions on topic and removes messages containing ideas already discussed.

In an unmoderated mailing list, all messages are automatically sent to everyone on the list.

rec.sport.basketball.pro

CHAPTER 15

Newsgroups and Chat

What is a newsgroup? How can I chat with others on the Internet? Find out the answers to these questions and more in this chapter.

INTRODUCTION TO NEWSGROUPS

A newsgroup is a discussion group that allows people with common interests to communicate with each other.

There are thousands of newsgroups on every subject imaginable. Each newsgroup discusses a particular topic such as jobs offered, puzzles or medicine.

Usenet, short for Users' Network, refers to all the computers that distribute newsgroup information.

The name of a newsgroup describes the type of information discussed in the newsgroup. A newsgroup name consists of two or more words, separated by periods (.).

The first word describes the main topic (example: rec for recreation). Each of the following words narrows the topic.

MESSAGES

A newsgroup can contain hundreds or thousands of messages.

Message

A message is information that an individual posts, or sends, to a newsgroup. A message can be a few lines of text or the length of a book. Messages are also called articles.

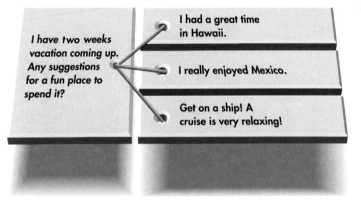

Thread

A thread is a message and all replies to the message. A thread may include an initial question and the responses from other readers.

NEWSREADER

A newsreader is a program that lets you read and post messages to newsgroups.

Microsoft Internet Explorer's Outlook Express comes with a built-in newsreader. Other popular newsreaders include MicroPlanet Gravity and Forté Free Agent.

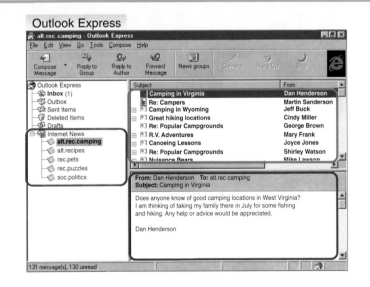

Outlook Express

■ This area displays a list of newsgroups.

■ This area displays a list of all the messages in the selected newsgroup.

■ This area displays the contents of a single message.

SUBSCRIBE TO A NEWSGROUP

You can subscribe to a newsgroup you want to read on a regular basis.

If you no longer want to read the messages in a newsgroup, you can unsubscribe from the newsgroup at any time.

Some newsgroups are moderated. In these newsgroups, a volunteer reads each message and decides if the message is appropriate for the newsgroup. If the message is appropriate, the volunteer posts the message for everyone to read.

Moderated newsgroups may have the word "moderated" at the end of the newsgroup name (example: misc.taxes.moderated).

In an unmoderated newsgroup, all messages are automatically posted for everyone to read.

alt (alternative)

General interest discussions that can include unusual or bizarre topics.

Examples include:

alt.fan.actors
alt.music.alternative

comp (computers)

Discussions of computer hardware, software and computer science.

Examples include:

comp.security.misc
comp.sys.laptops

news

Discussions about newsgroups in general. Topics range from information about the newsgroup network to advice on how to use it.

Examples include:

news.announce.newgroups
news.newusers.questions

rec (recreation)

Discussions of recreational activities and hobbies.

Examples include:

rec.food.recipes
rec.skydiving

sci (science)

Discussions about science, including research, applied science and the social sciences.

Examples include:

sci.med.dentistry
sci.physics

soc (social)

Discussions of social issues, including world cultures and political topics.

Examples include:

soc.history
soc.women

WORK WITH MESSAGES

READ A MESSAGE

You can read messages to learn the opinions and ideas of thousands of people around the world.

New messages are sent to newsgroups every day. You can browse through messages of interest just as you would browse through the morning paper.

PRINT A MESSAGE

You can produce a paper copy of a message you find interesting.

POST A MESSAGE

You can post, or send, a new message to a newsgroup to ask a question or express an opinion. Thousands of people around the world may read a message you post.

If you want to practice posting a message, send a message to the **alt.test** newsgroup. You will receive an automated reply to let you know you posted correctly. Do not send practice messages to other newsgroups.

REPLY TO A MESSAGE

You can reply to a message to answer a question, express an opinion or supply additional information.

Reply to a message only when you have something important to say. A reply such as "Me too" or "I agree" is not very informative.

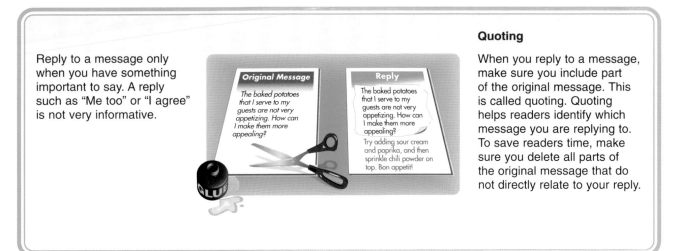

Quoting

When you reply to a message, make sure you include part of the original message. This is called quoting. Quoting helps readers identify which message you are replying to. To save readers time, make sure you delete all parts of the original message that do not directly relate to your reply.

Private Replies

You can send a reply to the author of a message, the entire newsgroup, or both.

If your reply would not be of interest to others in a newsgroup or if you want to send a private response, send a message to the author instead of posting your reply to the entire newsgroup.

NEWSGROUP ETIQUETTE

Newsgroup etiquette refers to the proper way to behave when sending messages to a newsgroup.

WRITING STYLE

Thousands of people around the world may read a message you post to a newsgroup. Before posting a message, make sure you carefully reread the message.

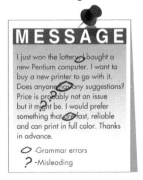

MESSAGE

I just won the lottery, bought a new Pentium computer. I want to buy a new printer to go with it. Does anyone has any suggestions? Price is probably not an issue but it might be. I would prefer something that are fast, reliable and can print in full color. Thanks in advance.

⌐ -Grammar errors
? -Misleading

Make sure your message is clear, concise and contains no spelling or grammar errors.

Also make sure your message will not be misinterpreted. For example, not all readers will realize a statement is meant to be sarcastic.

SUBJECT

The subject of a message is the first item people read. Make sure your subject clearly identifies the contents of your message. For example, the subject "Read this now" or "For your information" is not very informative.

Expensive Fishing Equipment

I really enjoy fishing, but all of my equipment is relat inexpensive. My fishing bu keep telling me to upgrad costly reels and lures. W actually make a differen is good technique mor than spending lots of

B.J. Wils

Hot Springs in Arkansas

My wife and I are planning to take a trip through Arkansas next year. We've heard ther are some lovely hot springs the state, but we don't kno where. Could someone p give us some advice?

Thanks, Mark C

Mountain Bike Tune-ups

This is my first year of mountain biking, and so far I've been doing my own tune-ups. But lately my bike hasn't performed well. For example, the chain slips when I switch gears. I'm wondering if I should pay a mechanic to do my tune-ups. Is it worth it?

Thanks, Ronald Hill

READ MESSAGES

Read the messages in a newsgroup for a week before posting a message. This is called lurking. Lurking is a good way to learn how people in a newsgroup communicate and prevents you from posting information others have already read.

READ THE FAQ

The FAQ (Frequently Asked Questions) is a document that contains a list of questions and answers that often appear in a newsgroup.

The FAQ prevents new readers from asking questions that have already been asked. Make sure you read the FAQ before posting any messages to a newsgroup.

POST TO THE APPROPRIATE NEWSGROUP

Make sure you post a message to the appropriate newsgroup. This ensures that people interested in your questions and comments will see your message.

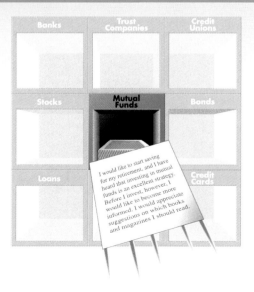

Do not post a message to several inappropriate newsgroups. This is called spamming. Spamming is particularly annoying when the message serves a commercial purpose, such as selling a product or service.

INTRODUCTION TO CHAT

You can instantly communicate with people around the world by typing back and forth. This is called chatting.

Chatting is one of the most frequently used features of the Internet.

You can use the chat feature to communicate with family, friends and colleagues in other cities, states or countries without paying long distance telephone charges.

Text-based

Text-based chat is the oldest and most popular type of chat on the Internet. You can have conversations with one or more people. When chatting, the text you type immediately appears on the screen of each person participating in the conversation.

Nicknames

People participating in a conversation often choose nicknames, so you should not assume that people are really who they say they are.

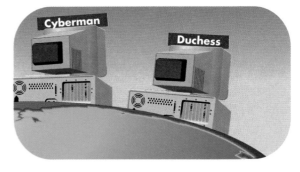

If another person is already using a nickname you want, you must choose a different nickname.

INTERNET RELAY CHAT

Internet Relay Chat (IRC) is a popular chatting system on the Internet. You can join a chat room, or channel, on IRC. Each chat room focuses on a specific topic, such as music or politics.

You need an IRC program to participate in IRC chats. You can get an IRC program at www.mirc.co.uk

WEB-BASED CHAT

There are sites on the Web that let you chat with other people. All you need to participate in Web-based chat is your Web browser.

You can chat on the Web at www.wbs.net

INSTANT MESSAGING

Instant messaging lets you chat privately with another person on the Internet.

You need a special program to participate in instant messaging. You can get an instant messaging program at www.icq.com

MULTIMEDIA CHAT

Multimedia chat lets you have voice conversations and communicate through live video over the Internet. You need equipment such as speakers and a video camera to participate in multimedia chat.

You can get Microsoft NetMeeting, a popular multimedia chat program, at www.microsoft.com/netmeeting

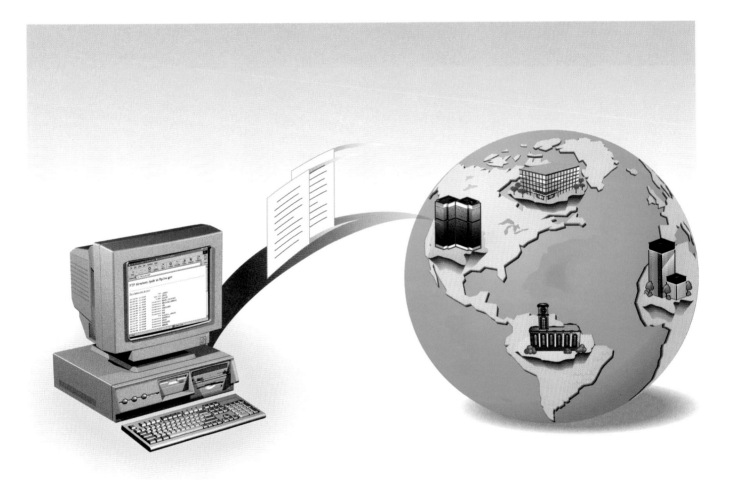

CHAPTER 16

FTP

What is FTP? This chapter introduces you to FTP and describes the different types of files you can copy to your computer.

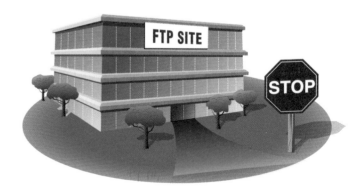

INTRODUCTION TO FTP

File Transfer Protocol (FTP) lets you look through files stored on computers around the world and copy files that interest you.

FTP SITE

An FTP site is a place on the Internet that stores files. FTP sites are maintained by colleges, universities, government agencies, companies and individuals. There are thousands of FTP sites scattered across the Internet.

Private FTP Site

Some FTP sites are private and require you to enter a password before you can access any files. Many corporations maintain private FTP sites to make files available to their employees and clients around the world.

Anonymous FTP Site

Many FTP sites are anonymous. Anonymous FTP sites let you access files without entering a password. These sites store huge collections of files that anyone can download, or copy, free of charge.

Files at FTP sites are stored in different directories.

Just as folders organize documents in a filing cabinet, directories organize information at an FTP site.

File Names

Every file stored at an FTP site has a **name** and an **extension**, separated by a period. The name describes the contents of a file. The extension usually identifies the type of file.

manual**.txt**

Development in the Western
sense is to
economy. |
Third Worl
production
especially
order to co
on the Wo
kind of de
however,
costly ma
expensiv
operation

porsche**.gif**

THE FTP SCREEN

FTP directory /pub/ at ftp.loc.gov - Microsoft Internet Explorer

File   Edit   View   Go   Favorites   Help

Back   Forward   Stop   Refresh   Home   Search   Favorites   History   Channels   Fullscreen   Mail

Address ftp://ftp.loc.gov/pub/   Links

FTP directory /pub/ at ftp.loc.gov

Up to higher level directory

```
10/19/94 12:00AM        144   names
08/09/96 12:00AM    328,315   INDEX
12/07/94 12:00AM      5,899   README
05/19/98 11:40AM   Directory  about.internet
05/05/98 09:38AM   Directory  american.memory
06/15/98 03:18PM   Directory  cds
02/19/98 12:31PM   Directory  copyright
06/18/97 12:00AM   Directory  crs
05/14/97 12:00AM   Directory  ead
06/07/96 12:00AM        374   exhibit.images
03/11/97 12:00AM   Directory  exhibits
12/12/96 12:00AM   Directory  flicc
08/04/97 12:00AM   Directory  folklife
06/04/98 10:22AM   Directory  gmdndl
```

Done   Internet zone

■ The files you want to copy to your computer are usually in the pub (public) directory.

■ Most well-established FTP sites include files that describe the rest of the files offered at the site. Look for files named "readme" or "index."

POPULAR FTP SITES

Some popular FTP sites include:

Library of Congress	ftp://ftp.loc.gov
Microsoft Corporation	ftp://ftp.microsoft.com
SunSITE	ftp://sunsite.unc.edu
Washington University	ftp://wuarchive.wustl.edu
Wiretap Library	ftp://wiretap.spies.com

The following Web site displays a list of most FTP sites:

http://hoohoo.ncsa.uiuc.edu/ftp-interface.html

TYPES OF FILES

There are many types of files available at an FTP site.

TEXT

You can get interesting documents for research and enjoyment, such as books, journals, electronic magazines, computer manuals, government documents, news summaries and academic papers. Look for these extensions:

.asc   .doc   .htm   .html   .msg   .txt   .wpd

IMAGES

You can get images, such as computer-generated art, museum paintings and pictures of famous people. Look for these extensions:

.bmp   .eps   .gif   .jpg   .pict   .png   .tif

SOUND

You can get theme songs, sound effects, clips of famous speeches and lines from television shows and movies. Look for these extensions:

.au   .mid   .ra   .snd   .wav

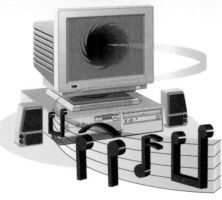

VIDEO

You can get movie clips, cartoons, educational videos and computer-generated animation. Look for these extensions:

.avi   .mov   .mpg   .qt

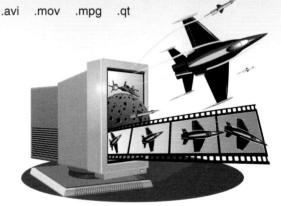

PROGRAMS

You can get programs to use
on your computer, such as
word processors, spreadsheets,
databases, games and much
more. Look for these extensions:

.bat   .com   .exe

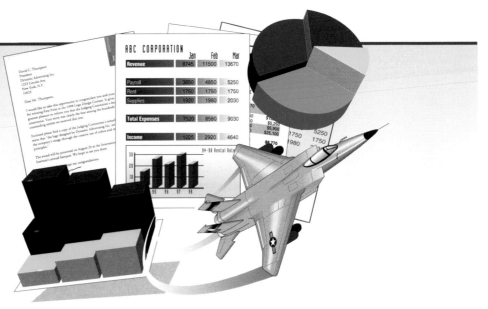

Public Domain

Public domain programs are
free and have no copyright
restrictions. You can change
and distribute public domain
programs as you wish.

Freeware

Freeware programs are free,
but have copyright restrictions.
The author may require you to
follow certain rules if you want
to change or distribute freeware
programs.

Shareware

You can try a shareware
program free of charge for a
limited time. If you like the
program and want to continue
using it, you must pay the
author of the program.

COMPRESSED FILES

Many large files stored at FTP sites are compressed, or squeezed, to make them smaller.

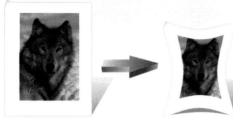

Compressed Files

A smaller, compressed file requires less storage space and travels more quickly across the Internet.

Archived Files

A program usually consists of a large group of files. Programs are often compressed and then archived, or packaged, into a single file. This prevents you from having to transfer each file individually to your computer.

Compressed or archived files usually have one of the following extensions:

.arc .arj .gz .hqx .sit .tar .z .zip

Decompressed Files

Before you can use a compressed or archived file on your computer, you usually have to expand or unpack the file using a decompression program.

You can often get a decompression program free of charge at sites where you copy files. Popular decompression programs include PKZip for IBM-compatible computers and StuffIt for Macintosh computers.

SEARCH FOR FTP FILES

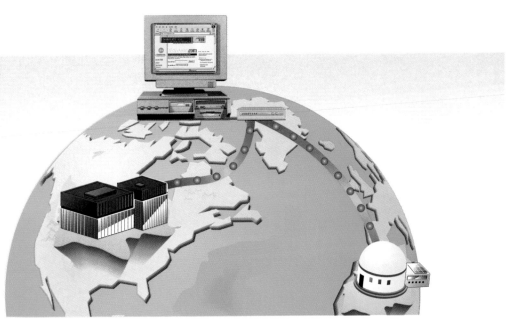

There are Web sites that let you search for files available at FTP sites around the world. This helps you find files of interest to you.

ARCHIE

Archie lets you search for specific files you have heard or read about. To use Archie, you need to know part of the name of the file you want to find.

Archie is available at:

NASA
www.lerc.nasa.gov/archieplex

Rutgers University
archie.rutgers.edu/archie.html

SHAREWARE.COM

Shareware.com lets you search for specific files or browse through files stored at FTP sites around the world.

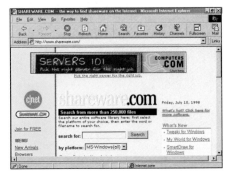

You can access shareware.com at:

www.shareware.com

FTP TIPS

AVOID TRAFFIC JAMS

Each FTP site can allow only a certain number of people to use the site at once. If you get an error message when you try to connect, the site may already have as many people connected as it can handle.

Connect at a Different Time

Try accessing FTP sites outside business hours, such as at night and on the weekend. Fewer people use the Internet at these times.

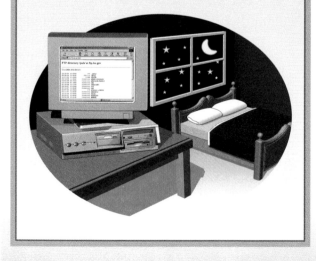

Use Mirror Sites

Some popular FTP sites have mirror sites. A mirror site stores exactly the same information as the original site but is usually less busy. A mirror site may also be geographically closer to your computer, which can provide a faster and more reliable connection.

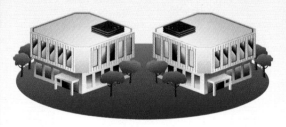

Mirror sites are updated on a regular basis to ensure that the files available at the original site are also available at the mirror site.

COMPATIBILITY

Just because you can transfer a file to your computer does not mean you can use the file. Make sure you get only files that can work with your type of computer. Many FTP sites have separate directories for Macintosh and IBM-compatible computers.

HARDWARE AND SOFTWARE

You may need special hardware or software to use files you get from an FTP site. For example, you need a sound card and speakers to hear sound files.

VIRUSES

Files stored at FTP sites may contain viruses. A virus is a destructive computer program that can disrupt the normal operation of a computer.

You should frequently make backup copies of the files on your computer and always check for viruses before you use any file copied from an FTP site.

Anti-virus programs are available at most major FTP sites.

INDEX

INDEX

Escape key, 28
Ethernet, 186
expansion
    card, 10, 16-17
    slot, 10, 16
extension, file, 153
    FTP, 265
external
    cache, 76
    modem, 52

F

FAQ (Frequently Asked Questions), 259
Fast Ethernet, 186
FAT32, 161
    convert hard drive to, 89
favorites, 205
fax, using modem, 51
fiber-optic cable, 183
field, in database, 136
    name, 136
file. *See also* document
    attach to e-mail message, 241
    compressed, at FTP site, 268
    extension, 153
    format, of images, 138
    name, 153
        FTP, 265
    path, 153
    save close captioning text as, 49
    store, on hard drive, 83
    types, at FTP site, 266-267
File Manager, 155
File Transfer Protocol. *See* FTP
find. *See also* search
    information in database, 135
    mailing list, 244
firewall, 188
fixed disk drive. *See* hard drive
flame, e-mail message, 239
flat file database, 137
flatbed scanner, 63
flat-panel monitor, 41

floppy
    disk, 90
        applications, 91
        choose, 93
        insert into drive, 92
        protect, 92
    drive, 11, 90-93
        in notebook computer, 116
FM synthesis, 61
font
    bitmapped, 38
    in desktop publishing program, 140
    resident, 38
    TrueType, 38
    in word processor, 129
food and drink, Web page examples, 224
form, in database, 136
formula, in spreadsheet, 133
forward, e-mail message, 241
freeware, 267
Frequently Asked Questions (FAQ), 259
FrontPage Express, 163, 207
FTP (File Transfer Protocol)
    introduction, 264
    screen, 265
    site, 264
        examples, 265
        how files are stored, 265
        search for, 269
        types of files at, 266-267
    tips, 270-271
full-duplex sound card, 60
function
    keys, 28
    in spreadsheet, 133
    switch, in mouse, 25

G

game
    considerations, 147
    controller, 146
    hardware, 146
    port, 15
    software, 146-147
GB (gigabyte), 7
Gigabit Ethernet, 186
glare filter, 44

INDEX

N

O

Original Message

I'm planning a trip to Rome this year. Any suggestions for sights I should see?

Reply

I'm planning a trip to Rome this year. Any suggestions for sights I should see?

I really liked the ancient Forum and the Colosseum.

INDEX

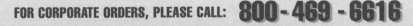

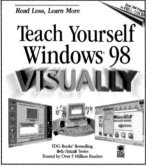

ORDER FORM

IDG BOOKS ®

TRADE & INDIVIDUAL ORDERS

Phone: **(800) 762-2974**
or **(317) 596-5200**
(8 a.m.–6 p.m., CST, weekdays)
FAX : **(800) 550-2747**
or **(317) 596-5692**

EDUCATIONAL ORDERS & DISCOUNTS

Phone: **(800) 434-2086**
(8:30 a.m.–5:00 p.m., CST, weekdays)
FAX : **(317) 596-5499**

CORPORATE ORDERS FOR 3-D VISUAL™ SERIES

Phone: **(800) 469-6616**
(8 a.m.–5 p.m., EST, weekdays)
FAX : **(905) 890-9434**

Qty	ISBN	Title	Price	Total

Shipping & Handling Charges

	Description	First book	Each add'l. book	Total
Domestic	Normal	$4.50	$1.50	$
	Two Day Air	$8.50	$2.50	$
	Overnight	$18.00	$3.00	$
International	Surface	$8.00	$8.00	$
	Airmail	$16.00	$16.00	$
	DHL Air	$17.00	$17.00	$

Subtotal _____

CA residents add applicable sales tax _____

IN, MA and MD residents add 5% sales tax _____

IL residents add 6.25% sales tax _____

RI residents add 7% sales tax _____

TX residents add 8.25% sales tax _____

Shipping _____

Total _____

Ship to:

Name _____

Address _____

Company _____

City/State/Zip _____

Daytime Phone _____

Payment: ☐ Check to IDG Books (US Funds Only)
☐ Visa ☐ Mastercard ☐ American Express

Card # _____ Exp. _____ Signature _____

maranGraphics™